*THE GIRLS ARE C...*

# MIDWEST  REFLECTIONS

**Memoirs and personal histories
of the people of the Upper Midwest**

*Eggs in the Coffee, Sheep in the Corn
My 17 Years as a Farm Wife*
MARJORIE MYERS DOUGLAS

*Dancing the Cows Home
A Wisconsin Girlhood*
SARA DE LUCA

*Halfway Home
A Granddaughter's Biography*
MARY LOGUE

*From the Hidewood
Memories of a Dakota Neighborhood*
ROBERT AMERSON

*Turning the Feather Around
My Life in Art*
GEORGE MORRISON
as told to Margot Fortunato Galt

*Barefoot on Crane Island*
MARJORIE MYERS DOUGLAS

*Shaping My Feminist Life
A Memoir*
KATHLEEN C. RIDDER

*Frederick Manfred
A Daughter Remembers*
FREYA MANFRED

**PEGGIE CARLSON**

# The
# Girls
# Are
# Coming

MINNESOTA HISTORICAL SOCIETY PRESS
St. Paul

MIDWEST REFLECTIONS
*Memoirs and personal histories*
*of the people of the Upper Midwest*

Publication of this book was supported,
in part, with funds provided by the
June D. Holmquist Publication Endowment Fund
of the Minnesota Historical Society.

For information, write to the
Minnesota Historical Society Press
345 Kellogg Boulevard West
St. Paul, MN 55102-1906.

www.mnhs.org/market/mhspress/

Manufactured in the United States of America

10 9 8 7 6 5 4 3 2 1

International Standard Book Number
0-87351-375-4 (cloth)
0-87351-376-2 (paper)

*Library of Congress*
*Cataloging-in-Publication Data*

Carlson, Peggie, 1951–
    The girls are coming / Peggie Carlson.
    p.   cm.—(Midwest Reflections)
    ISBN 0-87351-375-4 (cl. : alk. paper).—
    ISBN 0-87351-376-2 (pa. : alk. paper)
    1. Carlson, Peggie, 1951–
    2. Afro-American women—Minnesota—
       Minneapolis Biography
    3. Pipefitters—Minnesota—Minneapolis
       Biography.
    4. Minneapolis (Minn.) Biography.
    5. Sex role in the work environment—
       Minnesota—Minneapolis.
    I. Title.   II. Series.
F614.M59N43   1999
977.6'57900496073'0092—dc21        99-20893
                                         CIP

Lyrics from the song
"Come a Little Bit Closer,"
by Boyce, Hart & Farrell
© 1964/Renewal © 1992
by Morris Music, Inc.,
are reprinted by permission of
Morris Music, Inc., Los Angeles.

Cover photograph: Kent Flemmer
© 1999 by Kent Flemmer
Cover design: Will Powers

Author photograph courtesy
Minnesota Women's Press / Linda Cullen

*In memory of my mother,*
*Mary Jane Saunders Samples*

# Contents

*THE GIRLS ARE COMING*

# 1

## The T'ing

"GO GET ME DAT T'ING."

"Excuse me?"

"Dat t'ing. You know. Dat t'ing dat goes like dis."

I stared at Elmo. He waved five greasy fingers in the air. They looked like tree roots. I had no idea what he wanted.

We were bent over a maze of pipes in the boiler room of the Linden Building, a mile west of downtown Minneapolis and just south of the old Munsingwear underwear factory. Elmo was the foreman, and I was his gofer. He was the pipefitter, I the apprentice. I had been an apprentice for fifteen minutes and was already doubting that I would ever be a pipefitter.

"Could you give me a clue?" I asked, wondering how he expected me to know what a t'ing was. I was female, black, and unfamiliar with the intricacies of the Scandinavian workingman's dialect.

Elmo straightened up as if he had been bent over for several days. He moved unevenly, swaying from side to side. I braced myself for a barrage of insults attacking my femaleness. He said nothing. Instead, he adjusted his sagging dungarees, scratched his privates, and belched. I watched without reacting. I had spent the entire previous evening practicing apathy.

In the last days of spring 1974, I, Peggie Samples, was the first and only woman training to be a pipefitter in the history of the gas company. I had not begun my career at Minnegasco as a pipefitter trainee. Weeks earlier, I had debuted as Minnegasco's third female meter reader. A woman named Lila was the first female hired. Pam and I came on board shortly afterward.

The implied question put to the three of us was this: Can women be trained to do men's work? I knew the answer to that improperly stated question was yes, but unfortunately we had to prove it.

My stint as a meter reader was extremely brief because of a series of the most unpleasant experiences I had ever known, including an attempt on my life. I turned in my ring of meter-reading keys and decided to give a pipe wrench a try. If being a pipefitter wasn't an improvement over reading meters, I would simply go back to being a full-time college student instead of the part-time student I had become.

Elmo looked past me to a tangle of pipes and large tanks, which were connected to smaller tanks, which in turn were connected to more pipes hanging over our heads. The whole mess brought to mind beer bellies, pinheads, and too many arms—sort of like some of the guys I'd seen hanging around.

"We'll hafta get one a dem dere . . ." Elmo's voice trailed off thoughtfully. Then he noticed I hadn't moved. "Well, go on den. Whatcha standing dere fer? Go get me dat t'ing."

I left the boiler room and went to his truck. Elmo's truck looked just like him—filthy. Oily dirt clung to everything. Every type of t'ing imaginable was crammed into splintery wooden boxes or dangled from hooks and brackets.

I pulled on a pair of new canvas gloves and cursed myself for buying white painter's pants. Clearly a raiment faux pas. I began stuffing my pockets with pliers, wrenches, things that looked like cutting tools, screwdrivers of all shapes and sizes, and anything else that might classify as a t'ing. The tools blackened my pants and added fifty pounds to my weight. I grabbed twelve- and fourteen-inch pipe wrenches and, using my backside, slammed the van door shut. There was no doubt that by day's end I would be as filthy as Elmo and his truck.

I lumbered into the boiler room feeling sorry for myself. It was hot. Elmo stood with his head tilted to one side. Old sweat rings stained his shirt, and new ones were forming.

He scratched his head and squinted at something aloft, shading his eyes with an engineer-style cap. When he saw me he smiled.

"You're catching on," he said, pulling a pair of pliers from my pocket. "I'll take dis t'ing right here."

Elmo helped me over the language barrier. He explained that a "pounder" was a hammer. A "scroogie" was a screwdriver, as long as it was a flathead. A Phillips screwdriver was a "fancy scroogie." And so on. Flathead, scroogie, fancy scroogie, pounder. It wasn't difficult to see.

The t'ing he wanted was a Wilde pliers. Elmo did everything with a Wilde. He could break open a pipe, pick up a dime, or twist the cap off an aspirin bottle slicker than an eel. It was the only tool he really needed. Elmo slung his t'ing in the pounder loop of his pants. He whipped it out of there as if it were a six-shooter right out of a Hopalong Cassidy movie. I had visions of a sagging cowboy with the wrong hat.

Elmo and I banged around the boiler room, breaking open pipes and looking for obstructions. He carefully explained intake pipes, release lines, drainage systems, pressure valves, why this pipe ran upward and that pipe ran downward.

We found a dead mother mouse with six hairless babies still clinging to her teats, bobbing in loose pipe gunk. Elmo removed the rodent obstruction with his t'ing and flushed it down a toilet. I remained seemingly indifferent. No one would have heard my screams anyhow. The boiler room was so noisy, I worried about permanent hearing loss. Elmo rarely looked at me, so intent was he on his work.

"Gimme dat pipe over dere," he said. I found a length of pipe on the floor and handed it to him. He slipped it over the handle of the fourteen-inch pipe wrench that I had had the foresight to take from his truck. The fourteen-incher's teeth had a grip on a section of pipe. Wrapping both hands on the end of the pipe, he started to push. The line broke open with a pop.

"We call dat a cheater," he said, pointing to the length of pipe hugging the wrench. "Comes in handy when you ain't got enough torque to break her open."

"Her" was a reference to the pipe. Not to me.

Elmo pulled his engineer cap off and scratched his head, looking me up and down and grinning at my five-foot-four-inch, one-hundred-five-pound frame. Now what, I thought. I hated to be looked up and down like that.

"You're gonna need a lotta torque!" he said. Elmo scratched again and added sincerely, "S'long as a guy does his job, it don't matter ta me if he's a gal."

"Thank you," I said, feeling uncertain.

We finished working, loaded our tools back into Elmo's van, and headed for the Northeast Yard, our home base. I looked at the scruffy man who was somewhere between thirty-five and sixty-five years old and couldn't help wondering how I had landed in his moving pigsty, or on this job. I wasn't studying pipefitting at the university, and pipefitting couldn't have been more different from my previous

job as a student editor of independent-study workbooks. I
had seen Archie Bunker on television. I knew what to expect
from my new colleagues. They were from the "good ole boy"
set. No blacks need apply. No women, either.

The pace of my life had been relentless. I had arrived
home—in Richfield, a Minneapolis suburb—from boarding school, moved to Colorado, moved back home, moved
away from home, enrolled at the University of Minnesota,
married a grade school classmate, and ended up broke and
separated.

When a woman came to my apartment to install my
phone, I was surprised. I'd never seen a woman telephone
man. She told me that the *Big Three,* as she called them,
were going to have to start hiring women. "Equal Employment Act of 1972. The old boys are busy working Civil
Rights '64, and adding amendments," she said, flashing a
cocky smile. "We got to get instated fast because you know
as well as I do that the boys don't give it up because they
want to or because it's the right thing to do."

I nodded, feeling a call to sisterhood. I wasn't aware
of any employment act, but it sounded good. "The Big
Three?"

"Ma Bell, Northern States Power, and Minnegasco," she
said. My sister the installer told me what she made per
hour, and the next day I applied for employment with all
three of them. I knew nothing about the companies and
didn't expect to receive a response to my applications. All
three tested me and approved me for hiring. I threw a dart.
Minnegasco won, and here I was.

"Dere's lotsa colored people in my neighborhood, too," Elmo said. I wanted to ask him what color they were. It was my standard response to that remark. I didn't. Something told me not to.

"Don't mind 'em," he said, scratching his head and exposing oily tufts of hair while he steered the van with his free hand. "Coloreds are okay."

Let's have it, I thought. Whenever anyone starts with "So-and-sos are okay," it usually ends with "It's those other so-and-sos I can't stand." Who was it going to be this time? American Indians? Hispanics? Homosexuals? Had to be homosexuals. Minnegasco was man's country. Gays need not apply.

"It's dose goddamn kids!"

"Kids?" I was completely confused.

"College kids," he grumped. "Goddamn beer cans all over da place every weekend."

"Ah." This did not fit my stereotype of the working stiff. I ventured a guess. "Do you live near campus?"

"Yah, me and mama, we live dere now 'bout twenty-five years or so." For no particular reason, Elmo took his foot off the accelerator. The van practically stopped. "Me and mama, we brought up our two kids over dere. De're gone now." Elmo hit the accelerator, and we jerked ahead. "I got four grandkids!" A car honked and swerved around us. A hand with an extended middle finger appeared from a window. It was clear that for Elmo, driving and talking at the same time was a challenge.

Elmo had a big smile on his face. He talked about fishing

with his grandchildren and planting flowers for mama. He was oblivious to the pace of the world outside his van. I enjoyed listening to his stories, though I was concerned about angry motorists. Mercifully, we came to a red light. When the light changed, Elmo sped up to fifteen miles per hour, and we coasted into the Northeast Yard.

After he parked his van, Elmo disappeared. I went to find Lenny, my supervisor. Upon my arrival that morning, Lenny had explained that if I needed to use the facilities, I had to get from his office the pink WOMEN'S sign to hang over the blue MEN'S sign on the men's room door. "We fixed up a part of the men's room in case somebody's wife has an emergency. It's kind of a courtesy."

"Minnegasco's an all-male company," Sidney Wimple called from his side of the partition wall. Wimple was Lenny's boss. I was introduced to him at the same time I had met Lenny. Two things had struck me at that time: Wimple's name. And his clothes.

Sidney's tie looked as if it had had a recent run-in with a very ill infant. There were no words to describe its color. It was four inches wide and about six too short. His short-sleeved pink dress shirt, complete with white collar, was seeping blue ink from the breast pocket. I spotted a shiny polyester sport coat—olive green—hanging over a chair in his office.

"Yes, all male," Sidney repeated, pushing a huge pair of black-framed glasses over his small nose. He had to be farsighted; no one's eyes were that big naturally. "There aren't even any girl clerks, except for downtown where people expect that kind of thing."

I winced.

"No female secretaries," he said. "And no female . . ."

"Ah, Sidney," Lenny said, sounding worried.

"Bathrooms!" Sidney said proudly.

"Ah, but we're going to fix that part," Lenny said, blushing and focusing his attention on his shoelaces. Wimple vanished behind the wall.

"Which part?"

Lenny seemed confused. "Oh," he said finally. "The part about the bathrooms."

Not the no-females part, evidently. I stared a moment, wondering if I should suggest that they work on both parts. I decided against it, not wanting to jeopardize my intention to remain aloof and disinterested. "Thank you," I said, removing the pink sign from Lenny's grip. He sighed noisily and scurried away.

I went into the men's/women's room to wash the top layer of dirt off my face and hands. No emergency could induce me to sit. The plywood separating the men's side from the women's side was poorly constructed.

The women's side of the gnarled plywood was painted a heavy beauty-shop pink, like the sign. It was the sort of color that looked dreadful even when it was fresh. No way was it that color on the other side. The women's side had an antique toilet, the kind with a high mounted tank and a long pull chain. There was a rusty sink, a damaged mirror that reflected nothing, including my face, and a urinal that apparently couldn't be walled out. I wondered what they thought we'd use it for—a planter, perhaps?

I finished washing, took the sign down, and walked around to the "shop." The shop was the carpenter's workshop and the office watering hole. Constructing everything from custom-built desks and bookshelves to wooden stakes, filling out paperwork at the end of the day, putting equipment away, and gossiping were all the order of business in the shop. As I passed near a group of smirking gossips, I could hear stage whispers. *Women's libber. Radical. Lezzie. Too small.* I didn't respond.

Since I was not expected to do paperwork on my first day, I left the shop to have a look around. As I stood near a row of lockers, still holding the sign, a man moving too fast to be in Minnegasco's labor force walked toward me. He was wearing a pair of Levi's that actually fit. They showed definition in all the right places. I was certain he spent plenty of time in a gym. His light-blue work shirt was pressed and neatly tucked into his waistband.

I ran my hand through my hair. The first real stud I'd seen all day, and I looked like I'd just crawled out of a sewer. Mainly because I had. My mom had cautioned me about the dangers of becoming romantically involved with a colleague. Set your sights on neutral ground, and avoid having to work with an ex-"friend," as she put it. Given what I'd seen so far, Minnegasco was safer than a monastery. I liked to keep an open mind, though. The stud never would have recognized me as a female anyhow, except for the fact that I stood there broadcasting it by holding Lenny's stupid sign.

As he moved closer, I thought that he was probably fifty. What did I care? Plenty of twenty-two-year-olds dated older men. They didn't all live in Hollywood, either. His white hair was parted to one side, and its thickness rivaled Ronald Reagan's. He stopped in front of me.

"Elmo?"

Then, "Elmo," I said again. "You *really* look nice!"

Shop noise dwindled. Everyone stared at Elmo. Then at me. The sign pulsated—*Female tilt Woman tilt Sex tilt.* There was no place to hide. My face burned red. Apathy in the workplace faded.

A voice mimicked, "Ayl-mo-ow, you *really* look nice!" General hilarity.

Lord help me.

# 2

## *Dodging Nudes and Knives*

MY EXIT FROM METER READING was prompted by several events, none more terrifying than my encounter with the blue-haired lady.

But in order to follow the steps leading to the abrupt end of my meter-reading career, it's necessary to know some things about what Minnegasco was like before my arrival. When I was hired, management informed me that the company had a master plan that included hiring women into the Meter Reading Department but nowhere else. This meant nothing to me at the time, since I had no idea what one did in any of the other departments anyway.

Once I knew the names of some of them, I was glad that I had no other options. What did I know about Meter Repair, or Distribution, or Appliance Installation, or Buildings and Grounds?

"If female meter readers prove successful," the personnel guy said, "then you never know where women might be able to go in a company like this one." A big smile followed that statement. I worked up a little smile and waited for him to wrap up the pep talk. "And you," he finished, pointing a finger at me, "are special, being both female and black. You will help Minnegasco look good in two different categories."

I lost my smile.

But Minnegasco proved to be serious about hiring women into Meter Reading. Eventually, there were enough woman meter readers to form a softball team. The men's team was called the Minnegasco Flames. The women's team, I'm sorry to say, was called the Flamettes.

All meter readers, not just the female ones, were generally regarded throughout the rest of the gas company as being slightly better than grub worms. Meter readers weren't real laborers. They didn't wear tool belts. They ran from house to house, shamelessly hiding from dogs. They were taught to read meters from right to left, as if they were reading Arabic.

However, my departure from the job of reading meters had nothing to do with my low standing, or my lack of a tool belt. After one week as a meter reader, I was signing every job posting I could find, without bothering to read them first. My sole purpose? *To get the hell out of Meter Reading!*

As a meter reader, I was chased by packs of dogs, crazy canines dragging chains they had torn loose from iron posts. The dogs had one objective: *eat the meter reader!* I had doors slammed in my face by elderly women whose husbands told them never to open the door to a stranger.

Once I knocked on a door, and a male voice directed me to the basement. When I returned to the ground level to leave, I found him with another man, fornicating in the hall next to the door. Shock and confusion were stamped on their faces. I wasn't who they were expecting. I diverted my eyes and scooted past the lovebirds.

Earlier that same day, my supervisor, Mason, informed me that I had chosen my route—also known in the business as a "book"—well. "You got a permanently assigned book there," he said, pointing to the stack of preaddressed computer cards I was trying to stuff in my back pockets.

"What's a permanent book?" I asked.

"That book you're gonna read today ain't normally available to you rookies. One guy reads it all da time—same day every month—and he's probably off sick or on vacation or somethin'. I'd hafta check. It don't matter, though. Should be a easy day for ya."

Mason was right. It had been an easy day. I figured he was also correct about the route's belonging to a specific person, a person who probably wouldn't have wanted this particular book read by a rookie—especially a female rookie. It made a person wonder what was going on.

Permanent routes went to senior meter readers, not to rookies like me. Both the customers and the meter readers liked it that way. Customers felt more comfortable letting familiar faces into their homes. Meter readers had the advantage of getting to know the neighborhoods in which they were working, which enabled them to cut their workday hours, sometimes by as much as half. As a result, permanent routes were highly prized commodities.

I didn't read meters long enough to get one.

One day I was reading meters at the southern edge of the mostly white suburb of Minnetonka. I knocked at the back door of a big English Tudor and shouted, "Meter reader!" Loudly and clearly. I waited only a second before the door opened to reveal a naturally blond woman with fluffy yellow pubic hair and pear-shaped breasts. She was completely naked. To my open-mouthed stare, she calmly said that she was expecting somebody else. *Really?* I thought, recovering. *I wonder who?* I apologized for disappointing her and beat a hasty retreat, leaving the meter unread and the woman unserviced until the next month.

I was becoming suspicious that being put in the way of these sexual adventures might be part of some unofficial effort to make life at the gas company difficult for a new female employee. I found it particularly disappointing to discover that the man whose route I had read that day was one of the four black men who worked at Minnegasco. I'd spotted Washington the first day I arrived and was momentarily glad that I wasn't the only black person reading meters. But Washington made no effort to welcome me, so I kept

my distance. I didn't want him to think that I was his re-
sponsibility just because we were both black.

But Washington's lack of interest in me didn't last long.

The day after I'd met the naked Minnetonka lady, Washington was back from sick leave. He and Mason sidled up to
me. They both wore long, conspiratorial smiles.

"Have any problems yesterday?" Mason asked. He
wasn't even subtle enough to try to act concerned. The
two of them had obviously worked hard to set me up. Now
they anxiously awaited my reaction. They were so juvenile,
I almost felt sorry for them.

"Yes," I said. Their eyes widened in anticipation. "There
aren't any decent restaurants out there, and I didn't bring
my lunch." I shook my head. "From now on, I bring a sandwich." They looked disappointed.

On another suburban occasion, I had the misfortune to
step out of a bowling alley rest room and into the center of
an angry mob.

"There he is, officer!" A woman with bottle-orange hair,
wrinkled skin, and fiery blue eyes pointed a shaking finger
at me. "That's the man, officer! That gas man! He was in
the ladies' room! Arrest him!" Above the breast pocket of
her bowling shirt was embroidered LIL.

I felt the excitement mount among the bowlers. The
place was loaded with housewives. It was Ladies' Day.
These sisters probably hadn't had such a jolt since the
sump pump backed up.

"What were you doing in the women's room?" the officer growled.

I growled back, "I don't believe it's any of your business."

For the first time, the cop looked at my face. "My God, you're a girl!" he exclaimed. I said nothing. Then he inflated himself, turned to my accuser, and exhaled, "Lil, why didn't you look before you called me?" Turning back to me, he said, "Sorry, ma'am. We've obviously made a mistake." He crammed his notebook into his back pocket, spun on his heels, and stomped away, muttering. I was pretty sure I heard the words "Goddamn dumb broads." I assumed he was referring to the sisterhood of bowlers, not to me.

"How was I supposed to know she wasn't a guy?" the orange-haired lady whined to nobody in particular. "She was wearing a man's uniform."

"You're wrong," I said reasonably. "The uniform's mine. I own it. I'm in it. I'm not a man. Therefore, it's not a man's uniform." I looked pointedly at her bowling shirt. "Incidentally," I added, "the last time I saw a uniform like yours, the name above the shirt pocket was BOB. Aren't you the one in a man's uniform?"

If I had stayed in Meter Reading, the local cops would have had to hire a whole new squad just to handle me. The second time the police were called to protect the public from me was much more serious than the first.

Once again, I was working in Minnetonka. The day had been uneventful. Everyone had been fully dressed. Then, without warning, four squad cars, running silently, screeched to a stop, pinning me against a garage door. Four guns pointed at me, and nobody had to yell "Freeze!" since I was already frozen.

The cops claimed to have received a report from a citizen that a colored boy was casing the neighborhood, looking for houses to rob. Of course, it was ten o'clock in the morning on a lovely spring day, and the would-be robber, in a Minnegasco uniform, was knocking on doors and shouting "Meter reader!" for all to hear and see.

The cops must have thought this modus operandi was ingenious, for, much to my surprise, after looking at my Minnegasco picture identification, they insisted on calling the company to verify my employment before letting me go. So there I stood, with flashing red lights and cops everywhere, for thirty minutes, as passersby glowered at me. And then Minnetonka's finest departed, presumably—judging by the looks on their faces—to brood on how the world was changing for the worse. They offered no apologies.

These things didn't fill me with joy. But they weren't the watershed event that pushed me over the edge and started me blindly signing job postings. That event was the scariest of my Minnegasco career.

There was a cool breeze blowing that day, which made it particularly nice for walking. I had one block remaining on my route. I remember feeling pleased that only a few doors had been slammed in my face. Not a dog in sight. I felt like a veteran. Soon I would be home, soaking my feet in preparation for the next day.

Moving quickly, I made my way in and out of the final block of double bungalows on my route. All of the meters were inside, mounted in the basements, on the wall nearest the street.

"Meter reader!" I shouted, ringing the back doorbell of a home distinguished from its neighbors only by the white geraniums lining the sidewalk. I waited. Sometimes older people had trouble getting to the door.

"Who is it?" an elderly voice called sharply from behind the locked door.

"Minnegasco! I've come to read the meter!"

Slowly, about a dozen locks were unbolted. A relic with blue hair appeared behind the still-locked screen door.

"Meter reader," I said, smiling my most unthreatening smile.

"Who the hell are *you*?"

"Meter reader. Minnegasco," I said, pointing to the logo on my shirt. So far that day, people hadn't been greeting me like this, but I had been warned. *Pretend you don't hear the insult. Explain your business. Say thank you as you leave.*

The woman peered at me with steel-gray eyes. She had a long, pointed chin that she pressed to the door frame. "You're a *nigger!*" she snapped.

The words weren't new, but considering the kind of day I was having, they were completely unexpected. Recovering from the shock, I wondered if I was being tested—legitimately, this time—by the company. So I responded, "I'm a meter reader. I work for Minnegasco."

"I *told* them not to send niggers here!"

"They didn't."

"I don't like niggers!"

I'd had it, test or not. "Lady," I said, "I don't care much what you like or don't like. I'm here to read your meter. And

I've got a legal right to do it, and you've got a legal duty to let me."

Somewhere, this must have registered. Saying nothing, she slowly unlocked the last lock and stepped aside to let me in. "Hurry up," she snarled as I went by. "I'll be watching you."

*Not like I'll be watching you,* I thought. I found the meter easily and stood in front of it, shuffling my meter cards. The cards were sorted by address and supposedly packed by machine. Her card should have been at the top of the pack. It wasn't. It wasn't the second card, or the third.

"Nigger! What the hell are you doing down there?"

It wasn't the fourth card, or the fifth, or the sixth.

"Nigger! You better get the hell outta my house!"

Not the tenth! Not the eleventh!

"I got a knife, nigger!"

"Forget it, fool," I said aloud to myself. "You don't read this meter." With my hands shaking, I tried to stuff the pack of meter cards into my back pocket. They fell to the floor.

"I heard that!" she screamed. "Nigger! Thief! Don't think I can't tell what you're doing down there! I'm gonna call the gas company! I'm gonna call the police!"

*Call, bitch,* I thought.

I scooped up the cards, not bothering to put them in order. I crammed them into my pockets and turned toward the basement steps. I was sweating. I took a deep breath and put one foot on the bottom step.

"I'm leaving," I called, trying to make my voice calm. I waited for an answer. There was none.

"I'm leaving!" I called again, and peeked up the stairs. She was up there, all right.

"I got a knife! I'm gonna use it! You better get outta here, nigger!"

*Ho-ly shit.*

"All right," I said. "I'm leaving. Now. Just put the knife away. Put it away. And I'll leave." I carefully put my foot on the next step.

Now I could see it. It was a meat cleaver. She was swinging it around in a circle. They say a dog is less likely to attack you if you look it right in the eyes, so I locked eyes with her and started to climb the stairs.

"Stop!" she yelled, pointing the meat cleaver at me.

I stopped. We were both shaking. Loose skin wobbled under her bony arm as she struggled with the weight of the knife. She made a horrible retching noise and hawked a ball of phlegm at me. I tore up the stairs and grabbed the arm that was waving the meat cleaver.

"Get out!" she screamed.

I wanted nothing more. My right hand struggled to push the knife away from my ear. She jerked like a beast, trying to cut and slash. I jammed my knee against her and reached for the back door. The door was blue. Her hair was blue. An insane thought flashed through my mind: *Did she use hair dye on the door? Or blue paint on her hair?*

With my free hand, I reached for the door handle.

Locked. I was suddenly furious. I wanted to tear her face off. I wanted to scream racial obscenities at her, regardless of my upbringing. *You motherfucking white bitch!*

"Get outta my house!" she croaked. Spit flew from her lips. Her strength was waning. She had about fifty years on me, and it was starting to show. She wasn't any real threat to me now, as long as I could get the knife away from her. She had missed her best chance to hurt me by failing to throw the knife down the stairs while I was on my way up.

"Listen, dear," I whispered, my face inches from hers. Her breath smelled of rot and decay. "Drop the knife. Now!"

Old as she was, she fought with passion. It wasn't her physical strength that frightened me. It was her hatred. It was terrifying and enraging. I pulled her as close to me as I dared and glared into her eyes. "Drop the knife," I ordered, "or I will hurt you!"

The knife fell to the floor. Without loosening my grip on her arm, I kicked the knife down the stairs. For the first time in about a century, I breathed again.

But she wasn't done.

In a flash, she lunged forward and raised her hand as if to hit. I dodged, and she managed only to whack at air. She stumbled and fell toward me. I threw up an arm defensively. My elbow caught her under the chin, knocking her to the floor. I found the last lock, threw the bolt, and ran like hell: a half mile, maybe more, before I trotted to a stop. I sat on a curb, panting, and trying to collect myself, when I heard someone call my name.

"Peggie!" It was Mason!

Mason was skipping toward me. I could see that he was excited. I looked around for his unmarked spy car, but there were no cars in the area. He pulled up in front of me and started brushing leaves from his pants. It was rumored that he liked to hide in the bushes and spy on his readers. He tried to look concerned but failed miserably. "I just got a call from the shop."

Already? I couldn't believe it. He must have been in some nearby bushes. There were plenty. I noticed he had a walkie-talkie hanging from his belt, like a gun without a holster.

"We like to keep an eye on our new readers. In case they run into trouble. So I was in the neighborhood. In my car. My *company* car." So where had he hidden the company car? More important, how long had he been following me?

Liar! I fought to control my breathing, as he continued to brush thistles from his pants. He knew I'd find trouble at the end of this route. *I told them not to send niggers*, the old lady had said. At the moment, I hated him more than I hated her.

He stood there, now with a hint of a grin working on his face, waiting for me to fall apart. He could wait forever.

"They tell me you just had lotsa trouble. Seen ya running. That old bitch says you hit her." Now he was openly grinning.

"She lied," I said.

This man might have gotten me killed. Now the bastard

was trying to frame me. Hatred passed, consumed by rage. *Go ahead*, I thought. *Fire me. Then I can tell you what I really think!*

Instead, he looked disappointed. "Well, it don't matter anyway. She won't come to her door. I just tried. We had trouble with her in the past. She don't like niggers . . . sorry," he said, smiling, "I mean Negroes."

I said nothing.

"Well, so's everything okay? I mean, you were running." He looked hopeful.

"Must be uncomfortable in the bushes," I said. "Kind of tough to get all those stickers off your pants."

He stared at me for a minute. "Yeah," he finally said. "Well, as long as you're okay, I'll take off. You're almost done for today anyhow, right?"

Wrong again, pal. I'm done with Meter Reading forever!

# 3

## Inquisition

"ALL OF YOUR EXPENSIVE EDUCATION? For what? So you could become a plumber?"

Mom's huge black eyes enveloped me the way mothers' eyes sometimes do when they want to make you feel guilty about the money they've spent on you. When it came to money, Mary Jane Samples played the guilt card too often. Besides, I was grateful to my parents for making financial sacrifices to send my four brothers, two sisters, and me to Catholic schools.

My youngest sister, Jennifer, and I were bundled off to the Academy of Our Lady of Good Counsel, pushing the family purse to the limit. Good Counsel was an expensive Catholic boarding high school in Mankato, Minnesota. There I was supposed to be "finished" and prepared to take on significant things. According to Mom, there was nothing significant about fitting pipes, and I had just told her that this was my new job.

I stared past the bowl of fresh fruit on Mom's kitchen table. She stared back with deadly innocence. Mom was worried that her carefully laid plans were crumbling. Her daughter was studying to be a plumber, as she put it, instead of a journalist like her.

"I'm a pipefitter trainee, Mom. Not a plumber."

"Oh, what's the difference?" she whined. "Pipefitter, plumber, Northern States Power Company. They're all the same. They keep you from studying."

"I'm still in school," I said, wrinkling my brow. I was taking two evening classes each quarter, studying for a bachelor's degree in communications with a minor in history. She knew it.

Mom sipped coffee from her special thin-rimmed bone china cup. The cup was permanently stained burnt rose by Mom's lipstick. Late-morning sun shining through the kitchen window highlighted her naturally orange hair. She was a lady from the ground up. Graceful, if a bit plump, she was a mom who shouted softly, and who had read classics to us as small children. I knew she wondered how she could be responsible for producing a female pipefitter trainee. A mystery, I had to agree.

Mom had prepared lunch for both of us. I crammed a

corner of my tuna sandwich into my mouth. I saw her wince, but she held her tongue. Examining my sandwich, I noted the usual pickles, onions, celery, eggs, and mustard seed she loaded into every batch. She never allowed anyone near her food creations unless their skills were honed to perfection, by her. She was, I admit cheerfully, a willing, patient, and eager teacher. The way I was devouring her sandwich was sacrilegious. I didn't care. I licked my fingers clean and said, "Love your tuna fish, Mom!"

"Tuna *salad*, if you please. Not *fish*."

But I knew she wasn't interested in talking tuna. "That place where I work is *Minnegasco*, if *you* please. Not Northern States Power Company. And they aren't the same. Check your bills."

Mom was the person whom I admired the most—at least most of the time—but there were days when she tested my simple admiration. I wanted her support and empathy. I wasn't going to get it.

I wasn't going to get any support from my dad, either. By this time, Bob and Mary Jane Samples had divorced. Dad and his new wife, Pat, were busy setting up their newlywed home on the other side of town, in North Minneapolis. Dad's focus was on Pat. I didn't mind. I liked Pat a lot and thought it was kind of cute, especially at his age.

"What do pipefitters do?" Mom asked.

"Well," I said, "did you know that a pipe has no thread? You actually put fittings on nipples. Nipples are threaded pipes."

"I didn't know that," she admitted. "So why aren't you a nipplefitter?"

"You raise a point," I said. "Perhaps I'll ask, but not now. At this point I can't say words like *nipple* at work." Mom shook her head disgustedly.

I carried my dishes and napkin to the counter. I rinsed tuna and bread crumbs from my plate until it was almost clean enough to put back in the cupboard and stacked it with the other dirty dishes. I shook my napkin in the trash bin and returned to my seat still clutching it. Mom might have prepared dessert, after all.

She smiled approvingly, bit at a corner of her sandwich, chewed daintily, and swallowed. "So," she said, tracing the pattern of tiny blue flowers on her plate before completing her thought.

I waited, staring over her head at the china hutch full of beer steins and Hummel figurines my parents had brought to Minnesota from West Germany. (My father worked there for the State Department in the years just after World War II.)

Two fingers held Mom's coffee cup six inches from her lips, frozen in midsentence. She blinked. "You have been with Minnegasco since May?" she asked. This was one of those dangerous openings. She knew the exact date and hour that I started working at the gas company.

"Yeah," I said cautiously.

"And you have already needed to *escape*. Your word," she said, making a one-handed quotation mark in the air.

"You've had to escape from reading meters, and it's only June?"

"Yeah. So?"

"*Yes*, so," she corrected. "Does the gas company have enough departments to satisfy your flight pattern?"

I'd wondered how long it would take her to use my exit from Meter Reading against me in her constant opposition to my current employment. In a weak moment, I had given her a few details. Now she wheedled further information out of me as if she were on an assignment, conducting an interview.

"These guys deliberately sent you to this naked suburban lady?" Mom was gone: the woman before me was a journalist.

"Yes."

"How?"

"It wasn't hard," I said. "Every gas bill says when your meter will be read next."

"Mmm-hmm. Go on," she said, bobbing her head up and down. "I've seen the dates."

"Washington . . ."

"The black man?" she interrupted.

"The same," I said with disgust. "The blond was on his permanent route. All Washington had to do was to call her and remind her to be waiting. He probably said something real trashy, like, 'Hey, baby, daddy's coming. So be ready!' Some women like that kind of stuff, I guess."

"You mean he *told* her to answer the door naked?"

"Yeah. I figure she answers the door naked, and he gets a Minnetonka nooner." We both snickered.

"What about the homosexuals?" Mom asked, switching focus. "Do you think Washington sent you to them, too?"

"I don't think so, Mom. Word is, he's a lady-killer. I don't think I was supposed to meet the homosexuals. I think somebody else forgot to tell his friends that he wasn't working that day."

"And the blue-haired lady?"

"Oh," I said, shivering at the memory of that nasty relic. "That was a setup. Absolutely."

"Washington set you up?" Mom asked. "I don't like to think that any black person would do that to you, dear."

"It's odd, I know, Mom. But it's not my blackness that's an issue at Minnegasco. It's my sex. Anyhow, I'm sure Washington didn't act alone. Mason, the supervisor, was a player, too." I didn't have proof, but somehow I knew that the two of them had deliberately sent me to the blue-haired lady. I was supposed to have been scared right out of the gas company.

"I spoiled their fun, though. It normally takes about two years to get out of Meter Reading. I got out of there in a few weeks."

"Well," Mom said, getting in the last word, "you're not really out yet, are you, dear?"

When it was necessary, Mom and I ignored each other with practiced ease, as I did with her last question, which wasn't really a question anyway. She was interested, as a re-

porter, in my meter-reading story. As a mom, she was mad
that I had it to tell.

"I recorded the whole meter-reading saga in my journal."

"Recorded or not, I doubt you'll ever forget. I sure
wouldn't." We sat quietly for a moment, and then Mom
said, "Are you working near chemicals? Your color seems a
bit greenish."

"Mother!"

"Are we entitled to a discount on our gas bill?" she asked,
before I could object further.

"What do you mean *we*? I don't live here anymore."

"See what you can do," she said, ignoring me. "We deserve a discount." She stretched across the table and re-
filled my coffee cup with a delightfully impish grin. People
often mistook her for my sister.

"Your talents don't lie in nipplefitting."

New line of attack.

"Mmm," I said. "Where *do* they lie?"

"Certainly not in putting pieces of pipe together. College,
studying journalism, should be your full-time occupation."

She was a reporter for the *St. Paul Pioneer Press*, the first
black to hold that job on the paper. She wrote under her
maiden name, Mary Jane Saunders. It was her plan for me
to follow her there. As a family, we seemed to rack up firsts.
In 1951 we were the first black family to live in Richfield. In
1965 I was the first black student at Good Counsel academy.
Now I was the first female pipefitter trainee at Minnegasco.

"You only weigh ninety pounds," Mom continued, full

speed ahead. "How do you expect to handle all that heavy lifting?"

"I'll let you in on a little secret," I said, ignoring her attempt to convince me that she was ignorant of my true weight. "Nobody lifts a thing at the gas company. They have big machines that do the lifting."

"What about those muscle-bound Joes struggling with those giant pieces of machinery in the Ben-Gay commercials? Fakes, I suppose."

"Mostly, I'm afraid. I'm still looking, though," I said, remembering Elmo's transformation from grease monkey to white-haired stud.

I carefully pushed the bread crumbs from the table and into my waiting palm. "Did I mention how much I make?"

"*Earn*, dear. You're not *making* money, I hope?"

I rolled my eyes and leaned toward her with a Machiavellian smile. "Five dollars and forty-three cents an hour!"

"Sweet Jesus!" Mom whistled. "May I borrow twenty bucks?"

# 4

## Rockhead's Realm

MICKEY'S SMILE REMINDED ME of the snakes-in-the-Garden-of-Eden holy cards the nuns passed out for good behavior when I was in grade school. It was well past lunchtime, and Mickey and my current foreman, Rockhead, were playing a noisy game of cards.

I sat next to the cardplayers at a folding table in the middle of the Linden lunchroom, reading *Gaudy Night* by Dorothy L. Sayers. The poorly lit basement was damp and sticky. Rockhead called it a cafeteria, but the only food I saw on display was put there to kill a growing rodent population. The walls were a washed-out blue, with dubious-looking brown and green stains. Two dusty plastic rubber trees, one tipped sideways, were stationed in opposite corners. Presumably they were somebody's idea of decoration.

I turned a page of the mystery novel, holding it to cover my face. I attempted to make sense of the words as I hopelessly tried to ignore the discussion. Three weeks into Buildings and Grounds — B&G — and I yearned to be back under Elmo's wing. Elmo taught me more about pipefitting and using tools than I had learned in my entire lifetime.

When Elmo and I had finished clearing the sediment and grime from the cooling system in the boiler room, Lenny had sent Elmo on a one-man task and assigned me to Rockhead. Lenny said he wanted me to get a well-rounded education by working with each B&G foreman. Rockhead told me that he liked playing teacher. The only real lesson I learned from him, though, was how to repress the urge to murder him.

On Monday Rockhead ordered me to follow him to his truck. It was raining. He left me standing next to his locked van while he went to talk to "the boys," as he put it. I immediately went back into the shop, knowing perfectly well that I was supposed to wait for him in the rain.

"Where have you been?" he snapped at me when he returned, pointing a finger in my face as a father might scold a runaway child. I recognized Rockhead's voice: he was one of those in the shop who had heckled me when I first arrived. I was pretty sure he was the one who had called me a women's libber.

"When you left to talk to your boyfriends," I said, catching the slightest twitch in his eye, "I came back in here to get out of the rain. I know you aren't stupid enough to think I'd stand out there and catch a cold."

I gave him a moment to process the words. I didn't care what he might subject me to, now that he had lost his power game. "Are you done talking now, so we can go to work?" I asked sweetly.

Rockhead hiked up his tool belt, and we went to his van a second time. He reached past the steering wheel as if the act gave him great pain and turned the key in the ignition. The van jerked, and he pulled out of the yard at a pace that would have tested the patience of a turtle. Slow and slower seemed to be the driving speeds of choice at Minnegasco.

Rockhead drove through downtown Minneapolis, seemingly without purpose. Eventually we pulled to a stop in front of a six-unit apartment building on the Near North Side. The neighborhood was mostly black and poor. The building needed painting, a couple of windows, and some new front steps. Beer and pop cans and broken bottles and trash were scattered around the yard, and the grass was dotted with dandelions.

"I own it," Rockhead said.

"Own what?" I asked.

"The apartment building. It's mine."

"That building belongs to you?" I repeated, shocked.

He misread my astonishment as admiration. "Ya darn right, girlie," he said. "I got more, too."

I slumped down in the passenger seat of his van, embarrassed and fearful that some decent human being might see me. The rest of that day, Rockhead the Slumlord paraded me past the highlights of his miserable life as a provider of unsafe and shabby domiciles.

On Tuesday we went to a boat store, where he picked up his outboard motor from his cousin Bob, a repair guy.

Wednesday was the first of the month, Mother's Day to those who got welfare checks. On that day, Rockhead played Robin Hood in reverse, merrily collecting rent payments, robbing the poor of their slim pickings. Once again, I hid in the van.

Now it was Friday, cardplaying day.

"Truth is," Rockhead said, "the real reason there's so many fellows working here that's old enough to be this girlie's daddy is 'cus . . ."

"You mean granddaddy, don'tcha?" Mickey interrupted. Mickey's hair was white enough to qualify him as a granddaddy. He stubbed out a cigarette with yellowed fingers. Grinning from ear to ear, he slapped four cards down on the table and shouted, "Gin!"

"Read 'em and weep!" Mickey shouted, too loud for me to ignore. *Thank God it's Friday*, I thought.

Rockhead looked at the cards lying face-up on the table and pushed out his lower lip as if he were about to cry.

"Okay," he said. "Old enough to be her daddy and her granddaddy. It's because the gas company was the only company in the state hiring guys during the Depression. Ain't a one of us would be working here iffin it wasn't for that." He glowered at me. "A guy's gotta be obliging," he warned. "Even you."

Rockhead shoved his fingers into his pocket and pulled out two quarters. He flipped them, one at a time, at Mickey. Rockhead, I was to learn, carried a stash of quarters to handle his gambling losses. While he settled his account, I finished the last bite of my lunch and read another paragraph in my book. I wasn't interested in gas company history as told by Rockhead.

I had spent Friday morning in Rockhead's van, listening to his endless diatribes on every subject from the need for beef in my diet to the persecution of Richard Nixon by radical Democrats. As I sat in the lunchroom trying not to listen, I wondered if I was being punished for past sins.

Eventually, the cardplayers won my attention.

"Nepotism!" Mickey shouted. "Nepotism!" I gave up reading but continued to hold the book open to give the false impression that my attention was directed at it, and not at them. "Ne-po-tiz-zum is what we got to be grateful for, brother."

"You ain't my brother," Rockhead grumped, stressing *my*.

"In the eyes of God I am. You understand my meaning, I hope?" Mickey's voice boomed. He said *God* like a Southern Baptist preacher bent on saving the world from hell and damnation.

Rockhead winced. "There ain't nothing wrong with nepotism. We're family here. Bible says charity starts at home."

"Ah, but the Bible also says *Love your enemies*, and *Do good*, and *Lend money hoping for nothing gained*, and *your re-*

*wards shall be great.* And," Mickey nodded toward me, "it says, *Behold, I send you forth as sheep in the midst of wolves. But beware of men . . .*" Mickey consulted the ceiling and waved a hand dismissively. "Et cetera," he ended. "Matthew, sixteen and seventeen."

"Well, I'll be doggoned," Rockhead said, eyeing Mickey suspiciously. "Where'd *you* learn to talk like that? Everybody knows you're a goddamn atheist!"

"Yeah," Mickey said quietly. "I'm an atheist. A nonbeliever. A regular bad guy."

In the quiet that followed, I returned to my novel. I decided that I liked Mickey, if for no other reason than that he had silenced Rockhead.

During our week together, when he wasn't doing personal business, Rockhead had dragged me from one job site to another. He reported to as many folks as he could that "the girl" worked for him. At each stop, I was subjected to a litany of comments, suggestions, innuendos, and insults, since everybody seemed to know what was best for me. None of Rockhead's cronies seemed to have anything better to do. Finally, at the close of an emotionally exhausting week, we had landed, late, in the basement of the dingy old Linden Building for a dismal lunch.

The regular lunch crowd had long since departed to their jobs, and with them had gone the customary noise of a full lunchroom. I had thought, incorrectly, that the only sounds I would have to contend with were the shuffling of cards and the unsteady perking of a fifty-cup coffee urn that bubbled behind us on a counter.

As far as it is possible to feel sorry for an inanimate object, I felt sorry for that urn. It was clearly struggling with age and lack of care in order to prepare a lethal brew for the swing-shift workers soon to arrive. Whoever was supposed to clean it ignored the crusty brown and green stuff growing around it, and the box of rat poison stationed next to the box of stir sticks. But no amount of maternal instinct, or good-housekeeping tendencies, or fear of disease, or pity could have gotten me to act. The filth was going to stay intact, untouched by my female hands.

Mickey grunted out of his chair and zigzagged up to the urn on unsteady legs. He poured coffee and added a mound of sugar, spilling a good portion of it on the floor. I cringed. The Linden cooties must be living the good life. "Can I get you a cup?" he asked.

"Thanks," I said, too quickly. I meant to say, "No, thanks." Mickey set his cup down, rolled up his sleeves, wiped his hands on his pant legs, and got busy preparing a second cup identical to his own. I preferred my coffee black. He couldn't have known, though, because he didn't ask. He handed the cup to me, smiling politely and cautioning me to be careful because it was hot.

"Thank you," I said, dipping my tongue into the chipped porcelain. I managed to hide the shiver that went through my body. "Super," I lied. Mickey reddened slightly and went back to his seat, spilling more liquid delicacy for the cockroaches.

Not to be outdone, Rockhead stood up and hitched up his tool belt, grinning like an idiot. Rockhead burned more

calories hitching up his tool belt than he did doing anything else. It was past two, and we hadn't even looked at
a work order, let alone done one.

"Getcha some cream?" he asked, exposing a need for
dental work. Apparently his mother had neglected to tell
him that his teeth might turn green if he didn't brush. I
wondered what he was up to. This was his first attempt at
civility in the entire time we had been together.

Whatever the motive for his sudden change, I had no intention of discovering it. What I wanted from Rockhead
was to place as many miles between us as possible. "No,
thank you, Rockhead," I said. "I take my coffee black."

"Can't even treat some guys white," he muttered. "Oh,
'scuse me. I meant some ladies."

"Quite the contrary, Rockhead," I smiled. "I think you act
like a lot of white guys." Rockhead narrowed his eyes and
snorted.

The game was now cribbage. Mickey dealt. Rockhead
cut, and Mickey turned the cut card face-up. "Up jumped
the devil!" he yelled, flipping down a one-eyed jack and peg-
ging two holes. "The little spade gotcha!" he added, falling
into a fit of hysterical laughter.

After the week I'd had, the laughter was contagious, and
I joined him in spite of the fact that he'd just referred to me
as a *spade*. Rockhead's oxlike confusion made the joke easier to swallow.

Mickey wiped the tears from his face and cleaned his
hands on his pants. I thought, Who is this man in khaki
pants and a white button-down shirt? What does he do?
He seemed to have something to do with the meter-repair

shop next door and nothing to do with the second floor, where the offices with the men in the white shirts were. He didn't seem to own a pair of pliers.

Disregarding my intention to remain noncommittal, I asked him what he did.

"Mickey's supposed to be fixin' meters, but he don't do nothing but talk to his fricking broker on that telephone," Rockhead said, pointing to the phone hanging behind him on the wall. "Thinks he's a real big shot. Shit, Mickey, iffin you're so rich, what the hell's keepin' you here?"

Mickey leveled a stare at Rockhead over a pair of half-moon glasses. He rubbed his palm over his chin, appearing to be studying a serious problem.

"I enjoy beating the crap out of you," he said.

Rockhead blinked at the cribbage board as if blinking could change the results. He pulled off his stocking cap and rubbed his totally bald head. A rolling stone gathers no moss, I thought. Not everyone looks as good bald as Yul Brynner and newborn babies. People with piggy eyes and boulders from the neck up should invest in hairpieces, or wear big hats like Rockhead's. How misinformed my mother was to think that I could become romantically involved with a gasman, assuming they were all of the same species.

Mickey never did get a chance to tell me for himself that day what he did at Minnegasco, because Rockhead pushed away from the table and scrambled to his feet. He adjusted his tool belt around his sagging waist and motioned for me to follow him. He said he didn't feel like doing much more work. Much more? I would have been glad to do any at all.

Rockhead shuffled through his work orders and found an assignment to replace a broken window at an isolated regulator substation in St. Louis Park. When we arrived there, it was plain to see why he had chosen that particular work order. There was no one there but the mice.

# 5

## Circulating

AFTER ROCKHEAD AND ELMO, I was sent to work with "Box" Carr, the foreman who looked like a refrigerator.

"You ready for a tough day?" Box asked as we headed for the South Yard in his van. Minnegasco had "yards" all over Minneapolis and its suburbs, plus a multitude of small brick houses called regulator stations. I was slowly becoming aware of places that I had passed by for years without ever knowing what they were.

"Yup," I answered, trying to sound enthusiastic. The experience with Rockhead had left me apprehensive. "What are we doing today?"

"You know what a circulating pump is?"

Circulating pump. "A pump that circulates something?" I guessed, turning to look at him. There was more hair sticking out of his ears than there was on his head.

Box laughed. He pulled a pack of cigarettes from his shirt pocket and offered one to me. I declined. There was never any real danger that a natural gas leak would lead to an explosion and a fiery death in a Minnegasco van. But I wasn't too comfortable with the idea of smoking at work until I had been around long enough to have confidence in Gasco's nationally recognized safety record.

"A pump that circulates something," he repeated quietly. "I suppose that's what it is, all right."

When we arrived at the South Yard, we were met by a pride of lions disguised as men. They surrounded us as soon as we were in the building, all baring their dental work.

"Box, you square-headed old fart!" shouted a withered individual with sunken cheeks.

"Tiny, you and these guys don't look like you got any work to do," Box smiled. "You need any help?"

Tiny leered at me. He sucked on a cigarette, making his face look even more cadaverous, if that was possible. "I haven't needed any help since I was a little boy," he said, snickering. "Kind of a small harem you got there, Box."

"You'll never be so lucky," Box said.

My parents taught my brothers and sisters and me to fight with our brains and not with our fists. At that moment, though, I wanted to kick some serious butt. As Box and this clown jockeyed to one-up each other, I could feel the rest of the pride reveling, one moment in paternalism, the next in sexism. The one-liners continued to fly.

"I haven't needed any *luck* since I was a little boy, either," Tiny said.

"You seen your reflection lately?" Box queried smugly. The audience laughed in approval. Tiny, who reminded me of a weasel, shifted gears.

"I hope you brought your *tools* with you, Boxy. They tell me your *equipment* ain't been up to snuff lately." Tiny rubbed his nose and hitched up his pants, grinning. The lions roared. Tiny had scored big.

I had had enough. I stepped into the ring and looked Tiny squarely in the face. "Are you married?" I asked.

"Yah, me and the wife . . ."

"Do you have children?"

"Sure do," he said, hitching up his pants and looking around to make certain that everybody was enjoying his performance. "The wife, she knows how to . . ."

"Girls?"

"Three," he answered, suddenly cautious.

"Is this how you talk at home?" I asked.

The fun was over. The pride dispersed back to the jungle of Minnegasco's business.

I followed Box to the men's room, our job site. There was no point in getting upset with men like Tiny. There were too many of them, and I wasn't going to lose one precious minute of sleep over them. But I was mad that I'd let them pull me into the ring. I didn't want them to think I cared one iota about the things they said to me, or about me.

Before entering the men's room, Box took some cardboard from a trash bin and folded it until it was small enough to hang on the door. He pulled a grease marker from his tool belt, which was hanging over his shoulder, and wrote GIRL AT WORK. He stood back and examined his handiwork for a moment, frowning. Then he shook his head, turned the cardboard over, and wrote the words FEMALE AT WORK—STAY OUT. Satisfied, he took some duct tape from his tool belt and taped the warning to the door.

"That oughtta cause a run on toilet paper," he mumbled. Two men walked up to the door, stopped to read the sign, and walked in. "I rest my case," he said.

"Shall we ignore them?"

"I always do, whenever I can," he laughed, standing aside and holding the door open.

There was enough room to store a fleet of trucks in the men's room. It was enormous. The Northeast Yard women's room didn't even have an adequate partition. These men had two rows of lockers, six showers, eight toilets, and a dozen urinals. The middle of the room was dominated by a huge fountain, topped with flaking soap dishes. The fountain, Box explained, was a hand-washing station called a Bradley fountain. The Bradley looked like something out of ancient Rome.

In an out-of-the-way corner of the men's room, near the

back wall, hung a row of red circulating pumps, two of
which were not working. "Bad couplings," Box said. Fixing
the bad couplings was our business. We were hidden from
the room's other occupants but not from the usual rest
room sounds and smells. Tucked away there, Box, showing
no embarrassment, taught me how to take apart a circulating pump.

"The first thing to remember about taking anything
apart is, you put the parts down in the order that you took
them off," he said. "And to make sure you don't screw up,
you mark them with your grease marker. One, two, three,
and so forth."

Box pointed, and I unscrewed parts and set them down
in a line. Nut. Nut. Bolt. Bolt. Remove housing. Unscrew.
Unscrew. Remove coupling. We worked quietly. I did the
work. He instructed. Box said that my small hands were an
asset on a job like this. He said I would find it easier to ma-
nipulate the tiny parts and small motors than would most
of the clumsy, spatula-fingered guys. The replacement coupling slipped twice when I tried to twist it into place inside
the circulating pump. Box just smiled and said that sometimes it took him half a day to change a coupling.

"Look at these fingers," he said, holding up ten squared-
off stumps.

My fingers were long and thin. Piano hands, my mother
called them. I changed the coupling on the second pump in
five minutes.

"Good job," Box said.

I blushed. Box proved to be as instructive as Elmo, and

as patient. I tested his patience with a question. "How do you know when to change a coupling in circulating pumps like these?"

Box grinned broadly. "When the pump stops pumping."

What a strange place Minnegasco was. On the one hand, working with guys like Elmo and Box was pure pleasure. But working with Rockhead, and in Meter Reading with Mason and Washington, forced me to reexamine my motives for staying at Minnegasco.

There was the money, of course. I was aware that eventually I would graduate from the university and that my degree would present better, more fulfilling opportunities to make money. But until then, I was planted at the gas company and liking my paycheck.

Besides, what could I do with a degree in communications? My original plan was to write speeches for politicians. To get a better understanding of the territory I intended to work, I had volunteered in the 1972 McGovern presidential campaign. It didn't take long to realize that ghostwriting for politicians was not what I wanted to do. I never wanted to be held responsible for anything a politician said. But here I was, still a communications major, just riding the tide.

And if I were to stay at Minnegasco, I might be able to save enough money to pay cash for my education and leave the university debt-free. This was my actual plan. Unfortunately, the most carefully laid plans are always fouled up by life itself.

Once the Minnegasco paychecks started rolling in, I

signed up for a cooking class after reading that mercury was beginning to show up in tuna. This was of particular concern to me, since tuna represented a third of my diet. The cooking instructor said that no kitchen was complete without a few items, none of which I seemed to have. The total cost to equip my kitchen properly was more than two hundred dollars. I'd never known that cutlery was so expensive. In the end, I didn't have the patience to cook. In a week, it was back to tuna and mercury.

Next I had to buy a stereo set. Nobody had a hi-fi anymore. The salesman made it clear that once I heard the double-woofer four-foot-high quad-speaker mega-whoopie sound system—or whatever it was—spotlighted in his window, I would have to have it.

"When you can hear every last tap on the snare drum, you'll know you've arrived in music heaven!" the salesman said, ecstasy in his eyes, cupping his ear with fanned fingers while he listened to some private tune. I needed that sound system. Cost was not an issue.

The car came later. I had to establish a credit rating first. It came easily, once I became a card-carrying, non-probationary Minnegasco union member. As soon as I was able to borrow large amounts of money, salesmen stumbled over their words pitching car talk to me. As the debts piled up, it looked as though I might never get out of Minnegasco.

But I just loved my new blue Mazda. Zero to sixty in eight seconds. What power! I screeched into the Northeast Yard and came to a pulsating halt in the parking lot.

I sat in the car and let the machinery settle. Lovingly, I stroked the fake leather, and I waited. Everyone should have the chance to witness my entrance. They did. The car was surrounded.

"Pop 'er open," Box said, hanging on the passenger-side door.

I stepped out of my new car and slammed the door.

"Careful, baby," Sawdust the carpenter said, sliding into my seat. "She has to be handled delicately." He pushed the seat back to accommodate his legs. He adjusted the rearview mirror, winked at his reflection, and shifted the gears.

Greasy hands moved over my car. My—new—car! They were all smiling approvingly. Or frowning.

"How fast she go?" Box asked the windshield.

"Crank 'er up, Sawdust!" Sawdust turned the key. The hum of the engine brought whistles and catcalls.

"Whoo, mama! Listen, she's a bird!"

Bliss, the garbage truck driver, pushed Sawdust aside, taking over the driver's seat. He popped the latch, and heads disappeared under the hood.

"Lookee here, she's got rubber binders in here."

"And mice."

"Ain't this a Jap car?"

"Japan*ese*!" I shouted.

"Nothing made in America'd look like this."

"*Rotary* engine? What the hell's that?"

"Shit, Sawdust, it don't matter. Listen to her. She don't make a sound."

That was all I could bear. "The car," I shouted, "*my* car is a *guy*! Rex! R. Rex Seven!"

Several heads popped up from under the hood. I had been pushed out of the way and was standing a long distance from my Mazda. I was invisible. Hearing my words, the mechanics blinked and scratched before returning to their research.

"Rex," I heard Elmo say meditatively, above the din of a growing mechanical argument over the merits of U.S.-versus-foreign-made products. "Yah, she's a beauty fer shoore."

# 6

## Sonny Gets the Blues

MINNEGASCO WAS BLUE.

The walls were blue. The floors were blue. The uniforms were blue. The entire vehicle fleet was blue. Where there were curtains, even they were blue.

This may have been an attempt at color coordination, but I had my doubts. When I asked them, my four brothers and my dad said that their favorite color was blue. On a hunch, I asked Elmo and Box what colors they liked best. Without hesitation, they both said blue. It made me wonder what the world might have been like had baby boys been dressed in pink. In the interests of conformity, and of my private campaign to look just like everyone else, I bought several blue work shirts.

As a meter reader, I'd had to wear a blue shirt with Little Minnie, the company's Indian-girl logo, stitched to the breast pocket. I hung my Little Minnie shirts along with my plain blue work shirts in my closet, and I alternated wearing them throughout the workweek. The Buildings and Grounds Department was responsible for the maintenance and care of Minnegasco properties. Those of us who worked there had very little contact with the public, so we were not obliged to spruce up in fancy uniforms to impress people. Nevertheless, there was an unofficial dress code in B&G. It, too, was blue.

So on that day, early in the summer of 1974, when Sonny Kohn strolled into the shop wearing a skimpy electric-yellow halter top, every mouth fell open, including mine. Sonny was very tall and very blond, and gorgeous. Without doubt, she was not familiar with the unofficial dress code. She wasn't even wearing a bra, not that there was an official or unofficial code covering bras, so far. She was also wearing white painter's pants. Rookie.

Sonny scanned the frozen crowd with green eyes. She found me hiding between Box and Elmo. She smiled a crooked smile and bounced straight across the room as if she and I were alone and nobody else mattered. The men of B&G looked like they'd been poleaxed. Hormone levels were running dangerously high.

I knew Sonny well, though I had not known until that moment that she, too, had transferred to B&G. Sonny—

Jolene—was the fourth woman hired by the gas company. We met, of course, while we were reading meters. We had launched a campaign to stop the purchase of impractical "female" uniforms. Meter reading required that we stuff anywhere from fifty to seventy-five computer cards into our pockets and carry a large ring of keys belonging to customers who weren't at home during the day to let us in. We needed pockets and belt loops. The proposed new uniforms had neither.

Sonny and I went to Mason and complained. He said, "Hell, you gals will just have to make do. We got a professional designer all the way from Miami to design these little outfits for you."

"You mean that person who designs uniforms for airline stewardesses?" I asked.

"You bet," Mason said, walking around me to get a better look as I modeled the jacket, pants, and blouse, hoping he might see how foolish they were. "I think they're kinda cute."

"We don't want to be cute," Sonny growled. "We need pockets."

"Sew some on," Mason said. "You gals can sew."

"I don't sew," I countered. Mason wrinkled his nose.

"Where the hell are we supposed to hang our keys?" Sonny asked. She grabbed my arm. "These things have French-cut sleeves. I can't think of anything more ridiculous. We'll be snagging them on everything."

"You gotta wear 'em," Mason said, pushing out his lower lip.

In desperation, Sonny and I complained to anyone in a suit. Finally, we found Jack Hennessey. "I see," he said, after Sonny and I told him about the uniforms, including Mason's demands. "What would you suggest we do?"

"There's a guy reading meters who is two feet shorter than Peggie," Sonny said. "They don't seem to have a problem fitting him into a uniform. And if they can fit him, surely they can fit us."

Hennessey laughed. "You two go get yourselves uniforms from the company store," he said. "I'll sign the purchase slips and talk to Mason." He wrote order forms for the other two female employees, Pam and Lila, too, and handed them to us, still grinning.

Plainly, Sonny had not saved her meter-reading uniforms. The difference in how we were dressed was startling. In addition to my blue work shirts, I had bought a huge pair of bib overalls, Li'l Abner boots, and a red sweatband, which at that moment was sticking out of my breast pocket.

It occurred to me, standing there beside her, that I had done the best job of melting into a society of old white men that a young black woman could do without the help of fade cream. In fact, I felt as if maybe I had faded. I should have been happy. After all, with Sonny's arrival, I was not likely to be the constant focus of attention for a bunch of leering men. I shook Sonny's hand. "Good to have you here," I said.

The shop normally looked like the back lot of a long-forgotten junkyard. What appeared to be trash was stacked in teetering piles everywhere. Corners were cluttered with rotting wooden meter boxes filled with "parts" so old that nobody remembered what they were for. The shop smelled of stale tobacco and sweat, of Old Spice and axle grease. I liked it. It reminded me of my parents' garage after my brothers and their friends spent hours working on their rusty beaters.

Vacuuming the shop would have been hopeless. Dusting impossible. At that very moment, however, several guys started clearing the grimy Formica-topped table where we drank coffee and completed our daily paperwork. They were stacking ancient, well-thumbed auto magazines in corners. About a year later, Randy Ferrian—he was a fellow B&G pipefitter trainee, sympathizer, and peer—told me that copies of *Playboy*, *Penthouse*, and similar magazines had been removed before my arrival, by order of the management.

Sawdust found a work shirt and used it as a tabletop duster. He succeeded only in adding another layer of grime. A faded blue plastic flower arrangement appeared. Where it had been hiding, no one admitted knowing.

A glint in Sonny's eyes suggested that she was aware of the fuss being made on her behalf, but she did not concede that she knew. Instead, she stood next to me, asking endless questions in a loud voice. I answered in monosyllables.

"Is it better working over here?"

"Yes."

"You work in this place all day?"

"No."

"Meter reading sucked, didn't it?"

"Mmm."

"I told Lenny to call me Sonny, but I'm thinking about going back to my real name. You can't get up in a bad mood with a name like Sonny."

I grew more and more embarrassed as she spoke. All of the men in the shop were intent on capturing every word she uttered. I didn't want them to hear our conversation. I didn't want them to know what I was thinking, even about the most mundane things. I surmised that if they couldn't guess my thoughts, they would leave me alone.

"Peggie!" Lenny shouted. It was the first time he had called my name when he was handing out work orders. What now? Was I to be trusted to work on my own?

"Do you have any experience painting?"

Before I could answer, Sonny blurted, "Sure, we can paint." She put an arm around my shoulder. I caught a whiff of patchouli oil. She was a real hippie.

I was a four o'clock hippie, though I likened it to being an Oreo cookie—one thing on the outside, another on the inside. I wore bell-bottoms, but I thought they were ugly. I didn't really believe in free love. I tried marijuana, and a few other illegal substances, and didn't like them. I didn't believe that the idea of brotherly love originated with the flower children. Though I considered myself to be a radical, most radicals I knew were scary. The politics of Vietnam were confusing. Only the music was fabulous.

"G-G-Good," Lenny stammered, trying to look straight into Sonny's smiling eyes, and no lower. "I was planning to put you two ladies, I mean . . ." Lenny's ability to handle the politics of two women in his shop, challenged as he was by only one, seemed to be eroding.

Sonny winked at me. "*Ladies* is fine, isn't it?" she said. "I hope you plan to let us work together?" Her smile was wonderful. She would have her wish.

At that moment, I realized why I was embarrassed. Sonny wasn't the least bit intimidated by all the men. She was making me—standing there in my bib overalls—feel inadequate, foolish, and mad all at the same time. I felt unsure about my plan to use indifference as a way to get along. *She* wasn't going to hide behind indifference. Why did I? When had I become so cautious, or had I ever been anything else?

Lenny finally recovered. He cleared his throat and said, "Yes, I thought I'd put you ladies together for a while. So you can give each other support." He smiled uneasily, as I did. Sonny just smiled.

The new team was followed, cajoled, hit on, and harassed. Sonny and I entered buildings to the cry of "The girls are coming! The girls are coming!" Grown men, most of them fathers, chased us up and down halls with their arms outstretched and their lips pursed, making smacking noises. They promised us kisses we'd die for. Die of, more likely. I feared the excitement would never wane. Even after Lenny informed Sonny that OSHA required that she cover her, ah, *arms* while she worked, the crowds did not diminish.

Everywhere we went, groups of men stopped working to

watch us. When we painted the dock overhang at the Linden Building, a throng of avid onlookers witnessed every brushstroke. Eventually, Sonny grew tired of being on display. She climbed off the scaffolding and walked over to the men. "Is there something you guys want?" she asked.

Some said no. Some said yes. They all stayed. Frustrated, we pleaded with Lenny to put us on a different project, far from the masses. We were willing to do anything, as long as we could do it offstage. Lenny complied as often as he could. But his best intentions could not protect us from the need of many of the men to watch this new phenomenon called working women.

Another time, when the crowd was smaller than usual, Sonny approached one of the men.

"Have you ever seen a woman paint before?" she asked.

"Yeah," he said.

"Are we painting differently from what you expected?"

"I suppose not," he conceded, twirling his Minnegasco cap and looking everywhere except at Sonny.

"Then what's the attraction?" We waited, but he didn't seem to have an answer. A while later, he was back, watching.

Sonny and I had been working together for several weeks when we stepped out of the men's/women's room in the basement of the Linden Building. (Elmo and a contractor were working on a permanent arrangement for women, but they were far from being finished.) We found a pair of lacy black underpants lying on the floor next to the door. They definitely had not been there when we had gone in, only minutes earlier. A group of six grinning, beady-eyed lechers stood a short distance away, waiting for the show to begin.

Sonny picked up the lingerie, which had most likely been stolen from a wife, and strode up to the group. "Which one of you dropped your secret?" she asked, tossing the article of clothing in the air dismissively. I stifled giggles, my disgust vindicated. She winked at me, spun on her heels, and skipped down the hall with me in her wake.

Sonny and I soaked up as much information as we could on the road to becoming pipefitters. Although we painted and did other jobs that had nothing to do with qualifying for a pipefitter's license, we also spent plenty of time with the foremen. Elmo was the best of them. One day, in the Linden boiler room, I noticed that the pipes were all different colors, and I wondered aloud if this was just for the sake of variety.

"Shoot, no," Elmo said. "Da different colors tells ya what's runnin' t'rough da pipes. Ya see, da blue pipes is fer water, da yellow ones is fer air, and da orange ones is gas. Be kinda bad ta bust open da wrong one, don'tcha think?" He grinned. It was news to me, although I should have known that, if there had been a choice, they all would have been blue.

Sometimes Lenny would split up our team, sending Sonny and me to work separately with Elmo or Box or Rockhead. Elmo and Box became adept at shooing away unsolicited helpers, treating them like naughty boys. Rockhead, of course, encouraged them to stay. Under Elmo's and Box's guidance, I grew to appreciate my new craft. But as much as I liked working with them, I liked it best when Sonny and I worked alone.

"Got a boyfriend?" I asked Sonny one afternoon when we were able to avoid the spectators and have a quiet lunch by ourselves.

"No. There's nobody I'd want to lay claim to at the moment."

We were perched on the ledge of a wall surrounding the flat roof of the South Yard's main building. We were both wearing black rubber galoshes that came from the company store. That morning, Lenny had approached us, pinching the two pairs of boots in extended arms, as if they were poisonous.

"Gosh, I'm sorry," he said, "but the storeroom only has two sizes, large and extra large. We're gonna fix that, though, and order up some smaller ones." I hoped he was keeping a list of things that needed fixing.

Sonny and I were tarring holes in the roof that day. It was a job that required no special skills, but it wasn't easy. The tar had to be hot. It was already ninety degrees up there, and cooking tar made matters much worse. We were spreading the tar with flat shovels, sawed-off brooms, and window-washing squeegees. Our galoshes kept getting stuck to the tar and pulling off our feet. Tar stuck to everything. When I got tar on my face I wanted to cry. Fortunately, Lenny had given us a tube of goop that removed tar from the skin, and it worked. But everywhere it touched, it left behind an angry red rash. During lunch, the smell of the melting tar assaulted my nose, ruining the taste of my food and leaving me in a foul mood.

On the ledge, Sonny took off her work shirt. Underneath, she continued to wear halter tops. That day's white halter showed off a copper tan. Tiny beads of sweat trickled down her face. She arched her back, released her thick hair from a binder, and shook it down. She repeated this movement several times a day. I liked to watch the reaction it got when there were men around. I was sure she did, too. She pulled a canvas bag—complete with a toothbrush, a change of underwear, and her lunch—up on the wall. I took a tuna sandwich, an apple, and a Thermos of ice water from my brown paper bag and set them up on the ledge.

"Shit, it's hotter'n hell up here, and you want to talk re-*lay*-shun-ships?" She collected her yellow mane and tied it back in a neat ponytail. "Could be dangerous in this heat, but what the hell. Actually, I've known too many boys. I want to find me a man. You seen any around here?"

I thought she was probably kidding, but sometimes I wasn't sure what she was thinking. It didn't matter. I hadn't met anyone at Minnegasco who was ready for her.

"I don't think so," I said.

"Pity," she said, peeking inside her oversized purse and taking out a Tupperware container. "What about you? I see that ring on your finger. Is it real, or is it a decoy?"

I shifted uncomfortably. It wasn't that I was hiding the ring. I just hadn't expected such a direct question. "Both," I finally said. "I'm separated, but I'm not looking to add to the confusion. So I wear it to ward off potential problems. Not that there *are* any at Minnegasco. There isn't a lot of color around here, if you follow me."

Sonny laughed. "Color, wit, and youth all seem to be missing." I had no argument with that, but I was thinking about something else that had confused me since I started working at Minnegasco.

"I wonder sometimes," I said, "why it is that my race seems to be less of a problem for these guys than my gender. I mean, when I walk by people like Tiny and Rockhead and their buddies, I hear stuff like *lesbo,* or *libber,* or *feminist.* But I never hear *nigger.* I don't get it. When I started here, I thought all I would hear is *nigger* this and *nigger* that. I haven't heard it once—at least, not from these guys we work with."

Sonny sucked on a black olive. "You disappointed?" she asked. "Because I can assure you, *nigger* is what they're thinking. They're just too gutless to let you hear it."

"I know that. But I still think they're more bothered that we women are working here than they are about blacks working here. One of the reasons I think so is that the black guys haven't been very welcoming, either."

"You seen any black guys other than Washington?"

I took a bite of my tuna sandwich and winced. It tasted like tar. I wrapped it back in its waxed paper.

"Two janitors," I said, examining my apple. "One named Harvey. I met him the day I started here. The first thing he said to me was, 'Baby, this is no place for a li'l thang like you. You needs to be home fixin' to make your man happy.' You know, the usual BS. The other janitor, Jake, said he was a *maintenance engineer*, and he was worse than Harvey."

Sonny nodded. She worked on several more olives, rolling, sucking, and making them disappear. "So what happened?" she asked.

"What happened to what?"

"Your hubby?"

"Oh," I said, not wanting to be honest about the details of my failed marriage. "We fell out of love, I guess."

Sonny raised an eyebrow and turned her face to the sun. "That's original," she said. "So what *really* happened?"

I thought a minute, remembering the details of the fast marriage and the faster separation. Things had actually started to deteriorate during our honeymoon, but I didn't want to talk about it. "Bill and I were never really in love," I admitted. "We probably just wanted to get away from home. Kids, you know. Looking for freedom."

Sonny yawned.

"We were in lust," I added for good measure. She smiled her crooked smile.

"All right. We were parochial school classmates. We met in first grade. Funny how things turn out. I hated him then, but I didn't really get to know him until we were married. But that was the problem, wasn't it? I didn't really know him then, either. Too bad. We could have avoided a lot of unpleasantness. Bill turned out to be crazy, sorry to say. I mean quite literally certifiable. Very sad. How was I supposed to know he was that way? He seemed perfectly sane. At first, anyhow. Some crazy people are like that, you know. You can't tell. Especially from the outside. He is nice-looking. Tall. Slim. Great red hair. He wears it long. I don't want a divorce. We were both brought up Catholic, you understand. I feel guilty. Maybe I *drove* him mad. Like I said, he didn't seem nuts before we were married. He waited until we were on a mountaintop in Colorado to start showing signs of what his doctors diagnosed as schizophrenia. I could tell you stories. Anyhow, his doctors said he'd never get any better. I want a life, don't I? I'm still young. Right or wrong, I'm going to divorce him. I didn't drive him to schizophrenia. He was born that way. It's a strange life—when you live with a person who's getting messages beamed to him from the stars, you start questioning your own sanity. Well, believe me, I was relieved to learn that I had no part in making him crazy. It isn't my fault. His own doctors say I'd better divorce him, because there's no possibility of a normal life with him. I'm getting a divorce."

I stopped to breathe. For someone who wasn't going to talk, I seemed to have fallen off the wagon. I was out of control.

"You married your grade school classmate?" was all Sonny asked.

# 7

## Urbin's Ethnic Stew

AS FAR AS I COULD TELL, after a guy was hired by Minnegasco, he was sized up and then tagged with a nickname. Monikers like Rockhead, Box, and Bliss (for Don Blissenbach, the garbage truck driver) stemmed from their names. The electricians, one tall and the other squat, were called High Voltage and Short Circuit. They called the carpenter Sawdust. Minnegasco itself was reduced to Gasco, or MGC, or the Gashouse. Buildings and Grounds had so many names it was hard to keep track: B&G, Bungles and Goofs, and, with my arrival, Boys and Girls.

The tags were based on any number of different factors.

Elmo, for example, had simply been Mo until the episode with me left him stuck with *Ayl-mo-ow-you-really-look-nice*.

The extent of the damage I'd done became evident when Lenny handed out assignments on the morning of my second day in Buildings and Grounds.

Lenny sauntered into the shop with a cup of coffee and a big batch of work orders, studying them as if they were top-secret documents. He took center stage, cleared his throat, and shouted, "Robert! Al! Vern!" One by one the men went up for their daily assignments. Lenny didn't use nicknames, and nobody paid attention when he called out the names of others. Until he yelled, "Elmo!"

As if on cue, the entire shop crooned, "You really look nice!" I didn't find it the least bit funny, and I could tell that Elmo didn't either. Both of us were mighty grateful that within a week Elmo's new moniker proved to have too many syllables.

My nickname took a while to develop. It was clear that there was uneasiness with the obvious areas from which to develop it: race and sex. Most of the men, or the best of them anyway, hesitated self-consciously before even uttering words like *female* or *black*. The guys saying these words never looked me in the eyes. They wrung their hands, and their eyes twitched. They made *me* nervous.

In other situations, words like *gal*, *Negro*, or even *nigger* might roll off their tongues with ease. Around me, even the more innocent new terms took them some time to get used to. "Should I say *black* or *Afro-American*?" I was often asked. I shrugged, not really knowing, and not seeing much difference between the choices. "Should I say *woman* or *female*? Or is it *person*?" None of us was comfortable using these words in each other's company. This was odd to me, because nowhere else did I suffer from this sort of uncertainty.

"*Peggie* will do just fine," I suggested, much to everybody's relief.

Nevertheless, owing to a dispute over perceptions, I was given a nickname.

This dispute took place on a pleasant day. According to my journal entry, the sun was shining brightly, and it was a perfect day for painting outdoors. Being outside was a part of the work experience at Minnegasco that I truly enjoyed. I wasn't tied to a desk or a mound of paperwork or hovering bosses or high heels. I didn't have to paint my nails or add rouge to my cheeks or coordinate my outfit before I left for work every morning.

I was back with Elmo, much to my delight, and a new guy named Urbin Mayer. Elmo drove ahead in his own van to the job site. I rode with Urbin in a B&G fleet vehicle that was given to me so often that people referred to it as *Peggie's truck*. Urbin had been hired shortly after Sonny. He introduced himself by saying, "My name's Urbin Mayer. That's Ur-*bin*, not Ur-*ban*. It's no joke. My mom, God love her, didn't know what the hell she was doing when she christened me. Hell, I oughtta be running this town."

He spoke without taking time out for breath. He said it as if he'd said it a million times. I figured there was nothing

I could say that he hadn't heard already. I said, "Nice to have someone else in B&G who was born in the same decade as me."

I wondered how the guys were going to butcher his name. They didn't. Urbin was Lebanese. I shouldn't have been surprised when they called him Camel Jockey.

When I objected, he said, "It's no big deal. I'm just another terrorist from Nordeast, anyway."

"What do you mean, 'terrorist'?" I asked. "Did you and your friends throw rocks at cars when you were in junior high or something?"

"Yeah," he laughed. "That's a good way to put it. We were just a bunch of Nordeast bad boys, Lebanese-style. Ghetto kids with below-par educations. Most of us turned into dumb bullies, like me."

Urbin liked to call himself a dummy, but I hadn't seen any signs of it. "Is there a Northeast Minneapolis Lebanese ghetto?" I asked him. I knew all about the North Side ghetto, which was considered black, even though lots of other people lived there, too.

The expression on Urbin's face suggested that I was about to discover something that every Twin Citian above the age of two already knew.

"You're not from here, are you?"

"I am from Minneapolis, if that's what you mean," I said, knowing that my sheltered upbringing was about to be exposed, and not liking it.

"South?"

"Yes."

"How far south? South Bloomington? South of Lake Street?" he asked, with a smirk the size of an alligator's.

"Richfield, if it makes any difference." I hated to admit that I grew up in a suburb. People always jumped to conclusions.

"That figures," he said. "You don't sound like you got your education in the big bad city."

The Academy of Our Lady of Good Counsel was in a city—the small-town city of Mankato, way up on a hill, safe from all manner of riffraff, and guarded by the School Sisters of Notre Dame.

Urbin stuck a hand out the driver's-side window and pointed. "We are now in the Ukrainian ghetto," he said as we drove through a tidy, middle-class neighborhood that looked a lot like Richfield. The houses were older and the lots were smaller, but there were as many flowers and patios and two-car garages in this city neighborhood as there were in the suburbs.

Urbin explained that the Northeast Yard was in the Italian ghetto. Polish, Ukrainian, Lebanese, Irish, and Italian neighborhoods, among others, made an ethnic collage in Northeast Minneapolis.

"Everybody grew up a Roman Catholic, or a Greek Orthodox Catholic, or a Russian Orthodox Catholic, or a Uniate, or whatever. Hell, I figure Christ himself can't keep it all straight. Each church has its own school, too. Lotsa real estate in the God business." He laughed. "But," he said, "Nordeast ain't no melting pot."

I had always thought of Minneapolis as a big small town. I also thought I knew most of what there was to know about that big small town. I was humbled to discover that there was a whole community I knew nothing about.

"Where'd you go to school?" I asked, suddenly full of curiosity.

"Vocational. It's where they sent all the dummies."

"Where's that?"

Again, Urbin looked at me as if I'd come from another planet. "They keep you in a closet where you lived? It's downtown, or it was. I think it's a community center for the perpetually needy now, or a school for dancers, or some shit like that. Hell, what do I care?" he said, snuffing out his cigarette in the ashtray. "I didn't stick around. And I don't go back outta nostalgia, for Chrissakes."

Urbin was different from the other guys. It wasn't just his age. Or that he was fastidious about wearing clean shirts. Or that he washed his hands more often than I washed mine. He was secretive about his home life. I knew about his wife, Judy, but he kept his married life separate from work in a way that the others didn't. He referred to his wife as *Judy*, and not as *da wife*, which in itself made him unique.

One time, Urbin and I were called from a project that we were just about to complete and were sent to tackle an emergency air-flow problem at the Linden Building. Linden was a warehouse that had been partially converted to an office building, with meter repair shops on the top and bottom floors. Converted warehouses are notoriously problematic when it comes to heating and cooling. Warehouses by nature are big, open places. It is difficult to plug all the holes; they defiantly maintain their drafty spots.

When Urbin and I arrived, we were instantly surrounded by a group of folks with titles after their names. Engineer. Master engineer. Technician. Manager. Supervisor. Sidney Wimple and Lenny were among them. I saw Wimple first, in no small part because of his clothes. He was wearing a green plaid seersucker jacket and a red-and-white-striped dress shirt. His tie was navy blue, with flying yellow swordfish on it. I wasn't a fan of polyester bell-bottoms, but high-water bell-bottoms were particularly unattractive. Especially worn with white socks and shiny black wing tips.

Wimple and the others were shaking their heads and saying things like, "Ahem . . . aha . . . what you've got here is . . . system failure . . ." And so forth.

Urbin crooked a finger at me. "Hold this!" he said, popping a vent cover off its frame. The learned men watched suspiciously, with wrinkled brows, pursed lips, and pointing fingers.

With a flip of his wrist, Urbin pulled open the vent in question. The ensuing northerly breeze ruffled a couple of toupees. I stuffed my fist against my mouth to keep from laughing.

Urbin's geography lesson was the only interesting part of our ride that morning. He pulled my truck to a stop in the Brooklyn Park Yard. Elmo was waiting for us. We got out and padded over to where he was standing. Elmo looked around the yard, squinting. He put on a pair of glasses with thick black rims, removed his engineer's cap, and scratched his head.

"We gotta restripe dis parking lot," he said. "Brighten up da old stripes and make some new ones."

Elmo sauntered over to his van and opened the back end. He tossed a few things aside and then emerged with a tin of yellow chalk dust, a chalk line, and a tape measure. He pulled out the blueprint that was sticking out of his back pocket like a colorless fantail and unfolded it. He spread the blueprint out on the ground and invited us to have a look.

"See here?" he said, pointing to the edge of the paper. "Here's where we gotta put da new stripes. Dis here's da building," he said, pointing to a blue rectangle that represented the Brooklyn Park office, "and dese t'ings here are da trees and bushes. We'll be painting right here," he said, sliding his finger across the blueprint, opposite the office. "It's where we parked our trucks."

Urbin and I knelt next to Elmo, studying the blueprint. I had never used a blueprint before, but I found it easy to follow and an intriguing new adventure. Painting the parking lot might just be fun.

Elmo put the chalk line in my hand and explained how it worked.

"Measure the length and the angle of the space from top to bottom, according to the specs," I repeated after him. "Mark it top to bottom, run the chalk line across, then snap the line."

"Yah," Elmo said, scratching his head. "You got it!"

I took the chalk line and the tin of chalk and began to map out the new parking spaces. I was happy to be left to do this important surveying-and-marking job on my own. Working diligently, I drove the front tire of my truck over the chalky line to hold it still so I could snap it. I stopped from time to time to wipe chalky residue from my arms and hands and, ultimately, from my face.

Half an hour later, Urbin and Elmo rejoined me. Elmo carried a two-inch paint roller dripping with fast-drying yellow street paint. Urbin lugged an oversized wooden L-frame to guide the paint roller along the chalk marks.

Elmo looked quizzically at my lines. He turned to Urbin. "Whaddya make of dis?" he asked. Urbin shrugged.

"I don't get it," Elmo addressed me after strolling around my work. "Did ya use da tape measure?"

"Of course," I said, backing up to get a better look at my handiwork. I cocked my head to one side. The lines, I thought, were wonderful. I especially liked the way that the yellow contrasted with the fresh black asphalt.

"Well," he said, scratching yellow paint into his hair. "Either we been drinkin' or . . . Camel Jockey, ya ain't been drinkin', have ya?"

Urbin shook his head.

"Peggie," Elmo said, gently. "Dere ain't a single one a dem damn lines dat's right. How'dja do it?"

"Those lines are straight," I protested. "You guys aren't looking at them the right way."

I folded my arms across my chest and frowned as the

two of them dropped their striping tools and fell into fits of laughter. It was the only time I ever saw Elmo out of control. Eventually, they ran out of gas. Then, together, each using the other's shoulder for support, they hiked up their pants and tucked their shirts back in. By this time, I was showing teeth.

"Dem lines are straight, Peggie," Elmo said, "but how're ya gonna get a truck between 'em?"

I saw what he meant. Each of my lines was perfect in itself—but put them all together, and the pattern was wrong.

"Christ, Mo," Urbin said, wiping tears from his eyes. "She couldn't do the job with a plumb bob! Hey!" he shouted, as if he'd just thought of something brilliant. "That's what we can call her! Plumb Bob!"

The name stuck.

# 8

## Sonny Days

WHEN SONNY AND I FINISHED spreading tar on the South Yard roof, Lenny gave us another South Yard project. This time, we had to mount a stop sign and set it up next to the chain-link security gate.

At the Northeast Yard, Sonny and I loaded my van with a bag of cement, a wooden frame we had constructed from two-by-fours at the shop, and the new stop sign. We drove across town, talking all the way about Faye Dunaway and Jack Nicholson in the movie *Chinatown*, Gloria Steinem and the significance of NOW (the National Organization for Women) in our lives, and the shady behavior of our dishonest president, Richard Nixon. We talked passionately, especially about social issues. We agreed on most subjects. But when we didn't, more and more I found myself moving toward her way of thinking. She had lived a life, when I had only guessed about one. She grew up in a housing project. At sixteen, she left home to live on her own. At sixteen, I was in a boarding school, being told by nuns to be in bed by nine.

When we arrived at the South Yard, we got busy mixing cement and pouring it into the frame. We worked well together, each of us anticipating the other's movements. Sonny and I spoke very little, yet the work progressed at a steady pace. When we finished pouring the cement, we cleaned up the area and hosed it down. We returned the wheelbarrow, trowels, and water bucket to my van. Then Sonny and I took refuge from the heat under the only tree in the parking lot to wait for the cement to set. While we waited, we bolted the stop sign to its pole. When we had finished, Sonny took one end of the sign and I took up the other. We were about to march it to the cement stand when we heard loud voices behind us.

Several men were moving our way. They were pointing at us, jostling each other and laughing. Tiny was leading the band of hecklers. Waving a hand, he brought the group to a halt in front of us. They effectively blocked our path.

Tiny stood facing me, his emaciated frame reminding me of a neglected house plant, dry and withered. He made a great show of examining our work, circling around us, and nodding his head approvingly. He dipped two fingers in his shirt pocket and pulled out an unfiltered Camel. He tamped it against his hand, lit it, and blew a wobbling smoke ring that hovered over his head like a tainted halo.

Sonny dropped her end of the sign and moved to stand next to me. She followed every one of Tiny's movements with her eyes, her mouth twisted into a nasty grin.

"Lookee here, my friends," the small man wheezed. "I do believe these girls here had themselves a stroke of in-*gee*-nee-us." He pushed his hands under his belt and rocked on his heels. The road-map veins in his eyes rivaled those in his nose. I suspected that he drank as much as he smoked.

I said nothing, having made a conscious decision not to try to reason with him. Sonny thought my plan was for cowards.

"Sign's standing up right as white!" Tiny said. "And it ain't even backwards!" Laughing and choking, he spat a thick yellowish blob of phlegm that landed at my foot. I wanted to run like hell, but I stood rooted to the spot. I dropped my end of the sign. It crashed. Tiny flinched.

The five boys with Tiny were smart enough to recognize fighting words. Their joy was evident. I was beginning to think that they were all welded together. They laughed as one, single-minded in their appreciation of good-ole-boy humor.

Sonny stepped directly in front of Tiny, crowding him, leaving him no choice but to stand his ground or retreat. She raised a palm in a gesture of confusion and smiled sweetly. "I don't see any girls here, Teeny," she said. "Where do you see the girls?"

"Girlie, if you don't know whatcha are, you better run home and ask your daddy. On the other hand," Tiny said, blowing another wobbly smoke ring, "Ol' Tiny here'd be mighty glad to explain it to you." He nodded at the boys and leered at Sonny.

"Listen, little boy," Sonny said, pointing a finger at Tiny. "And you must be a boy, 'cause they sure don't make men in *your* size, now, do they?" she scoffed. "I doubt you could explain crap to a toilet, but that's not the point," Sonny said, smiling again. "Point is, I know who I am, and I also know *exactly* what *you* are!"

Tiny whipped the cigarette butt from his mouth. His lips dropped apart.

"Listen, bitch," he growled.

"Careful, Tiny," one of the welded-together boys said. They knew it was not okay to use the *B* word. They had been forced to attend sensitivity-training sessions, where they were given a truckload of words they could no longer use. As if this wasn't bad enough, they were also given a big list of new words they were instructed to memorize. Words like *women* and *black*.

Tiny sucked on his cigarette, spitting and coughing. He yelled, "You goddamn bitches should be home doing women's work. You must be lezzies or something. We don't need you here!"

Sonny smiled sweetly. "Oh, dear," she crooned. "It's lesbians, isn't it? And you say you don't need us? Have we caused you discomfort? I am sorry. Our only wish at this time is to negate belligerence and antagonism. But I must insist that we establish proper nomenclature before we proceed *en avant*. I'm afraid the use of the term *bitches* is really rather puerile."

Tiny blinked.

"It means 'childish.'"

*Bravo*, I thought, feeling a growing affection for the enigma beside me, and wondering how she would surprise me next.

With shaking hands, Tiny pulled another cigarette from his pack and lit up. No smoke rings this time. "Who you callin' belligerent?" he asked, fully understanding the meaning of *that* word.

"Why, you, sir," Sonny said, her voice changing. "But understand these words, if you can. I'm here to stay. And the next time you call Peggie or me a bitch, you might be wondering where your next paycheck is coming from."

Tiny narrowed his eyes and coughed.

"Come on, Tiny," a band member said. "Let's get outta here and go ta lunch. I think she's smarter'n you." He pulled at Tiny's sleeve, and Tiny allowed himself to be led away.

Sonny and I watched them all go. Eventually, we picked up the stop sign and resumed working. "By the way," I said, "where did you learn to talk like that?"

"In the projects," she said.

After a while, when I wasn't working, or at home, or in school, I was at Sonny's place. Like me, she decorated her apartment with old things, handmade things, and one-of-a-kind things. She had a jungle of potted plants, mismatched kitchen chairs, tapestries, hand-sewn quilts, braided rugs, and an antique claw-foot oak table. Sonny had a good eye for color, and though she was far from wealthy, her apartment never gave a hint of her true financial situation.

One night in late fall, we were drinking tea and eating Sonny's homemade, sugarless, honey-filled sugar cookies in her apartment. "You know," she said, looking at me, "I can't figure you out. You were up there on that hill in Mankato with the nuns for four years. Did they take all the spunk out of you, or what?"

"No," I said. "They actually put some back in. It was St. Richard's grade school in Richfield that took it all out. The kids, anyhow. Actually, I got a lot of good things out of Good Counsel."

"Like what?" Sonny asked.

"Girlfriends, for one thing. You see," I explained, "aside from my sister, who is five years younger, I was the only black girl at St. Richard's. I wasn't popular. I didn't have friends there. But the very first girl I saw at Good Counsel came running up to me, shouting, 'Oh, a Negro!'"

"Didn't that piss you off?"

"Not at all. The next thing she said was, 'We're going to be best friends.' I'd just come from a place where nobody liked me because I'm black. And this girl was saying she was going to be my best friend—because I'm black."

"And what happened?"

"Well, of course I was suspicious. I thought she was weird. She wanted a black friend. And I wanted a girlfriend of any kind. As it turned out, we would have been friends anyhow. We're still best friends."

Sonny stretched across her couch and bent her elbow under her head.

"You've heard me talk about Mugs, Mary Ann, and Barbie Joe Kelly," I said.

"Many times. Hope to meet them in person, someday."

"You will. But they're all Good Counsel graduates, too. We became friends for life on that hill. Their friendship kept me wanting to go back for four years—they are the reason I liked it there—even though there were no boys to fight over, or other black girls on campus."

"Really?" Sonny said. "I would guess a black friend would have been extremely important to a sixteen-year-old. Especially in a town as white as Mankato."

"Probably, Sonny. But don't forget why I went to Good Counsel—I went to make friends. I was looking for girls to laugh and plan parties and sleep-overs with me. And friends to share my secrets and favorite novels. Skin color didn't seem so important at the time."

"I know what it's like to be lonely. It just seems to me it would have been nice if one person up in that isolated, cloistered community had the same kind of hair as you!"

Sonny had a way of always being right. It both annoyed me and endeared her to me. This time she was missing the point, though. Sex and race are never far from the surface of any issue for black women. Yet sometimes—not often, but sometimes—they fall second, as they did in my search for friendship.

"Again, perhaps," I said, acknowledging that hair *is* important to sixteen-year-old girls. "But don't assume this make-believe black girl and I would have been best friends just because we shared the same heritage. Besides, Good Counsel was a lot of fun."

Sonny still wasn't convinced.

I sighed. "Junior year, I ran for student council president."

"You, taking up politics?" Sonny said. "I can't see it."

"Yeah, well, things were different back then," I said, tapping out a cigarette.

"Good Counsel wasn't the real world. The place was *The Trouble with Angels,* Hayley Mills: four nuns and a guitar perched on the altar, wailing for the love of Jesus so out of tune it was painful. La la land. Like this place.

"Anyhow, the election results were announced. I won. The very next day the principal, Sister Ann Marie, calls an all-school assembly. I'm thinking she's going to introduce the new officers and drape a sash over my shoulders, or something." The image was vivid in my mind. "I still burn whenever I think of what she did that day."

I bit my lip, pushing back the tears that threatened my resolution never to cry again. "'Electing a student council president is very serious,'" I said, mocking Sister Ann Marie's voice. "'The election should not be based on a popularity contest. Therefore, a new election will be held immediately.' I wasn't even president for one day. After the nun tallied the second set of votes—all by herself, I must add—I lost.

"I cried for days. I quit doing homework. The nuns didn't even care. I didn't eat, or sleep much. Mugs said I looked old. I was so embarrassed, I wanted to crawl home. But I stayed. And when I stopped crying, I got mad. Especially when Sister Ann Marie introduced the Student Congress, a new organization that had to have a president. The nuns unanimously voted me to be it. Surprised?"

"They threw Student Congress at you to make themselves feel better?"

"That's exactly what they did."

Sonny and I sat quietly for several minutes, listening to Bob Dylan singing "It Takes a Lot to Laugh, It Takes a Train to Cry."

"I hated them for making me president of the Student Congress," I said, eventually. "The pieces weren't all there, but I knew the stench of racism. Anyhow, the president of the newly instituted Student Congress didn't do a damn thing, except to get her picture taken. Every time the school paper did a photo of the organization heads, there I stood, right behind Terry Schramski, the proper student council president."

Shaking her head in disgust, Sonny took one of my cigarettes and lit it. "You're wrong about one thing," she said, finally.

"I am?"

"The real world truly was up on that hill."

# 9

## Predator in a Van

DRIVING SOUTH ON I-35W through downtown Minneapolis and the suburbs of Richfield and Bloomington was endless and monotonous, until we reached the bridge over the Minnesota River. There the scenery changed from uninspiring architecture to trees, open skies, prairie grass, and the river.

A steady rain pounded the van's windshield. It was the kind of cold autumn rain that cut deep and chilled to the marrow. I had acquired a Minnegasco letter jacket, and I was glad to be wearing it.

I was working with JE (pronounced *Gee)*. His real name was John Ellan, but everyone called him JE. I had worked with him twice before, when he helped Elmo and me reroute heating ducts at the Linden Building. JE had said very little then, and he spoke even less that day as we drove southward. We didn't actually have any conversation. He simply grunted and gestured in my general direction. That was fine with me. I preferred not having to respond superficially to conversation that bored me.

Once we were over the bridge, I loosened up. I hadn't realized that rush-hour traffic wore so heavily on my nerves. Feeling better, I smiled at JE and at the plastic Jesus he had mounted on the dash of his company van. Neither smiled back.

JE reminded me physically of Box. He had the same square body and the same thickness about his limbs. He was taller than Box, and I think he had more hair. But it was impossible to tell what was happening underneath the stocking cap that was apparently glued to his head.

Earlier that morning I had asked JE where we were working. "South," he said. Answering a simple question with more than one word was evidently a problem for him, or, more likely, the problem was my race or sex. I did not intend to ask which it was. Instead I shrugged off his curtness and made a mental note not to ask questions. I had assumed he meant the South Yard, which everybody referred to as South. But the South Yard was miles behind us, and I could not fathom our destination until I saw the giant Little Minnie logo in the distance. Then I knew exactly where we were going: I had often seen this logo on family trips to Iowa.

Later that day, I learned that the station (where the big Little Minnie with the blue flame feather overlooked the Minnesota River valley) was called the Dakota Station. JE turned off the freeway in the opposite direction from Little Minnie and the Dakota Station.

He drove on in eerie silence. The sound of speeding traffic was replaced by the banging of tools against the metal cabinets in his van. The giant logo disappeared behind us, and we entered a wooded area. I sat there enjoying the wide-screen view, marred only a little by the exploding raindrops.

I wondered why the gas company had put a meter-regulator station in such an isolated location. There were no industries out here, no homes, no building sites. A dump spoiled the landscape on the other side of the river. There were leafless trees, with abandoned nests, and damp ground covered with fallen leaves. Red squirrels leaped from piles of twigs and scampered up and down trees.

JE turned again, this time toward the edge of the river, onto a stretch of road that was no more than two dirt tracks barely the width of the van. We were close to the water, and flocks of geese fluttered and honked as we intruded upon their domain. He continued along the path next to the river, and I saw that the maples, oaks, and pines had increased in size and stood closer together. I was reminded of the red-hooded girl who found herself alone in the woods with a wolf. And then I knew.

I turned my head a hair's breadth. I was certain that JE saw my eyes, searching for an explanation from him. Yet he stared straight ahead and said nothing, keeping both his hands wrapped tightly around the steering wheel while small beads of sweat trickled down his face from under the black stocking cap.

Heat from the van's blower blasted my face. I broke into a cold sweat. My eyes darted wildly. Usually I was adept at knowing where I was. Not this time. I was totally lost. Trees I had been enjoying became bars in a cell. Birds squawked. I ran my fingers along the door frame and found the lock. The sound of my unlocking the door was lost in the noise of crashing tools and the truck's engine. I wanted to scream, but who would hear me?

"Where are we going?" I said, in a voice unfamiliar to me.

For an answer, JE pulled into an open space where the trees had been cleared. He stopped the van and undid his seat belt, then turned and faced me. His movements enveloped my thoughts like a black hole in a nightmare. I thought, *If you touch me, I'll tear the stick shift out of the floor and . . .*

Still JE did not speak. But his breathing was loud and uneven. His steely eyes peered at me. We were frozen. Wired. It felt as if my body had been turned into stone. I could not move.

It rained harder. I tried to reason where I might run if I could find a way to break free from the animal beside me, whose breathing fogged the windows. There was no place to go. I pushed back tears that might make me more vulnerable than I was already. I knew that if I broke down, he would have his way.

How could I have been stupid enough to think that I could work with these people? *You asked for it*, everybody would say. Foolish girl. What did you expect from a company full of men?

*If he moves, grab a hammer*, I told myself. But I'd have to reach past him to get a hammer. Besides, he probably had a hammer of his own, or a wrench, or a utility knife.

*Kick him where it hurts*, I told myself. But how? We were sitting in a van. *Run like hell*, I told myself. Where to?

His breathing slowed, and became gravelly and raspy.

I prayed. *Our Father*... Stop. Another man. *Pray!* I commanded myself. "Hail Mary, full of grace," I said softly. "Blessed art thou among women."

I heard the key turn in the ignition and the engine rumble so loudly I thought I might scream out with joy. "Hail Mary, full of grace," I repeated a little louder, not daring to look at him for fear he might turn off the engine again. I squeezed my eyes shut, trying to recapture the intensity of my Catholic school days. "Holy Mary, Mother of God, pray for us sinners, now and at the hour of our death," I finished. *My death*, I thought, pushing away the image of myself fighting a losing battle against him.

Hate unlocked my frozen limbs, and I stared at him with dangerous eyes. *Drive!* My eyes demanded what my voice would not.

JE drove out of the clearing and back onto the road. "Amen, dear God," I whispered. "Amen."

The van smelled of rotten sweat. I wrinkled my nose and turned away from him. My cheek bumped the window glass, and I realized that I occupied only a quarter of the passenger seat. I did not move.

We entered Dakota Station through the east gate, taking a winding road to the main building. I jumped from the van and ran into the building while the van was still moving into its parking space.

A cluster of men sat around a folding table, drinking coffee and smoking cigarettes. They looked like farmers, dressed as they were in dirty bib overalls. Most of them wore red bandanas wrapped around their necks. I thought if I untied the scarves, heads would roll. An invisible string pulled their faces toward JE as he followed me into the room. A second passed before one of them spoke.

"Oh, Geee-eee," he said, drawing out the *E*s and laughing. Everyone greeted JE that way, and they all seemed to think it was funny no matter how many times they'd heard it. "What da hell is that little thing you got with you?"

That brought a fresh round of laughter from all, except for JE. He remained silent, studying his shoes. I stormed past him and slammed the door. I stood outside in the rain, against the wall, overcome by disgust. I cried convulsively, gulping for air. My hands shook as I struggled to light a cigarette. The nicotine did not ease the pain, so I dropped the cigarette in the mud and stomped on it again and again.

Above me, Little Minnie loomed, no longer friendly. *I told you so. I told you so. I'm the only girl who's safe here*, her mocking smile seemed to say. I checked my watch. It was 9:30. I would have to be with JE, working beside him, following his instructions, riding in his filthy van, for six more hours.

Normally I didn't chain-smoke, but I took out another cigarette and lit it. I could call Lenny and ask him to come and get me because I was sick, I thought. But JE was the sick one. And what would I say to Lenny? "JE stopped the van and . . . he looked at me! No, he didn't touch me, but . . . but he threatened me! He frightened me!" Would Lenny understand? Would he even believe me?

I didn't make the call. I went back into the building, to work.

"Why the hell didn't you tell me?" Sonny shouted, a month after what I came to call "the JE incident."

"I was afraid you might do something crazy," I said.

"I'm not the one you had to be afraid of," Sonny said, waving her hands in my face. "JE's the one acting crazy."

"I know," I said. We were sitting on plastic folding chairs in the backyard of her apartment building. It was one of those late-fall days you like to take advantage of, because you know that the temperate weather isn't going to last. A small patch of Michaelmas daisies flourished in a corner of the yard where Sonny had planted them.

"At least that explains why you've been acting so strangely," Sonny said. "JE walks into the shop, and you walk out. Lenny hands out work orders, and you're in the corner, looking all sad." Sonny glared at me. "You told Lenny, didn't you?" she shouted.

"No," I said. "You're the only person I've told."

"But Lenny knows. He must. He never sends you with JE anymore."

I thought about the way Lenny had looked at JE and me when we returned to the shop that day. "Maybe he does know," I said.

"JE's probably been bragging about it," Sonny said angrily.

"To whom?"

"To all of them. He's probably got them all thinking they can do it, too. Screw the black chick."

"Be serious," I said. "Nobody screwed anybody. Anyway, if he'd been bragging to everyone, just about the entire male component of Minnegasco would be peering at me, looking for a mark. They'd be whispering in corners and propositioning me at every turn. And you, too, of course. I can't believe how often I get mistaken for you." I shook my head. "I don't think he's told anybody anything."

Many times, I had thought of telling my mother, or Lenny, or Sonny, but didn't. I knew there were laws against what JE had done, but they seemed vague and unhelpful. I didn't think they covered a ride in the woods. Every time I played the incident over in my mind, I couldn't think of anything concrete he'd done wrong. He had just frightened the hell out of me. Was that against the law?

"You know," I said, "I don't understand JE. He acts like he's embarrassed or something. He never looks at me anymore. He acts as if he's scared of me."

"Scared of you?" Sonny asked, smiling. "I'm the one he

oughtta be scared of. Hell, if it'd been me, I'da grabbed his . . ."

"No," I interrupted. "You'd have been just as scared as me. The guy's got two hundred pounds on both of us. Don't think I'm not still mad, though. I have nightmares," I added.

"I'm not surprised, Peggie," Sonny said. "Tell me about them." She lit a cigarette and pushed the straps down on her halter top, trying for the last of the sun to maintain her summer tan. I wondered, in passing, why so many white racists spend their summers trying to get darker, and how they have nothing else in common with my friend.

"It's one of those fast-moving nightmares," I began. "I'm being chased by this giant bear."

"A giant bear with JE's ugly mug, I bet."

"Sometimes it does seem as if the bear has JE 's face," I said. "The bear is monstrous, bigger than any bear I know of. His mouth is wide open, and slobbering. Just as he reaches me, I wake up. It takes me a while to figure out I was only dreaming. It's been cutting into my sleep."

Sonny threw up her hands in disgust. "He can't get away with this. There must be something we can do."

"Like what?"

"Get the bastard fired. Or sue the shit outta him. Jeez, what he did's got to be illegal."

"Take it easy," I said. "You know as well as I do it's my word against his. They'd say stuff like, 'Why did you wait so long to tell us? You didn't act like anything happened.

You didn't even tell your best friend. Hell, according to you, he didn't even touch you.' Nod nod, wink wink. That would be more sickening than I could take—to be humiliated a second time."

For a long minute, Sonny and I sat quietly.

"Damn," she said finally. "It's so *wrong*."

# 10

## The Induction

AS TIME WENT ON, the men I worked with seemed to fall into two groups—the Elmos and the Rockheads. To my relief, there was nobody else like JE. The Elmos ranged from individuals who were quietly curious about the phenomenon of females in the workforce to those who were only interested in how we did our jobs. The Rockheads were less complicated.

I kept a running tally in my journal, and I shared my ideas with Sonny. I learned, not surprisingly, that she was engaged in a similar analysis, with similar results. Her groups were the Yahoos (the Rockheads) and the Regulars (the Elmos).

The surprise was that there were more Regulars than there were Yahoos. Some of the Elmos, we agreed, were even attractive guys like Urbin, Elmo, Randy, Lenny, and a number of others, including some who even lowered their eyes and blushed shyly whenever Sonny and I were around. Those guys treated us with old-fashioned courtesy.

I thought these things, and then I worried about thinking them. *Shy, courteous, attractive*—these were dangerous adjectives when I applied them to my coworkers. They were the kind of sentiments that could lead to relationships. For me, a Gasco romance would most likely be a gain-a-lover, lose-a-mother proposition. Besides, there were other, more decisive social reasons why I could never be involved with a gasman.

First, I didn't fish. The idea of jabbing a live creature with a hook and then feeding it to yet another victim never appealed to me. Minnegasco-style fisherpersons, I was told, fished while simultaneously battling mosquitoes and drinking beer—lots of beer. Participating in any of these activities was not how I wanted to spend one minute of my free time.

Second, I didn't hunt. The only difference between hunting and fishing, I gathered, was the absence of beer during the killing part. As far as I could tell, even the biggest boozers didn't mix shotguns with Schlitz. I should have been grateful for that, I guess. On the other hand, leaving Bambi motherless seemed far more brutal, and much bloodier, than scaling a sunfish. I had never held a gun, and I never would.

Fishing and hunting were as Minnegasco as the color blue. It seemed that every man in the company enjoyed the following pieces of property: da cabin, da lake, da snowmobile, da house, da garage, da car, da dog, da t'irty-ought-six, da wife, and da kids. It was hard to tell if these things were listed in order of importance or preference. In any event, I was not interested in becoming "da wife."

Still, no amount of self-discipline could overcome the workings of nature. It was impossible to ignore the fact that there were men at the gas company. New, younger men were being hired, as were new, younger women, though not as many and not enough. With fresh young male faces, it became increasingly difficult to stay focused on changing filters in air-handling units, digging out sludge from drainage systems, and running new pipelines. Except when I was working with Rockhead. Then it was easy to stay focused.

From time to time, it was still necessary for Lenny to send Sonny or me on a job with Rockhead, even though Lenny understood why we disliked working with Rockhead. He also seemed to sense the tension between JE and me, and for the most part I did not work with JE.

While we were sitting in the Linden lunchroom on a break, I asked Sonny, "Do you think it's time we asked Lenny not to send us with Rockhead anymore?"

Sonny thought for a moment as I sipped my coffee. I'd stopped seeing all the brownish gunk around the coffee urn. It got so I even liked the coffee, though I started taking it with plenty of cream and sugar.

"Not yet," she finally said. "Our six months aren't up yet. I think we should wait until we get sworn in at the union meeting next week. Then let's do it." I agreed.

Sonny and I—and Pam and Lila, who were still reading meters—were all scheduled to be sworn in together. I had to admit that my knowledge of unions came solely from history books and movies. Unions seemed deliciously raffish. I imagined smoky halls with back rooms where deals were cut, radical leaflets left on folding chairs, and men sloshing beer in mugs as they sang the "Internationale" in halls decorated with red flags.

At the Wednesday-night induction, the Local 340 pipefitters sang a halfhearted version of "God Bless America," followed by the Pledge of Allegiance. I was disappointed.

Don Ryder, the union president, sat at the center of the dais at the front of the hall, surrounded by the other union officers and the executive committee. All men, of course, and all white. Ryder took several seconds to scan the crowd. His gaze came to rest on the four of us. We're all here and ready, I thought. He nodded, pulled at his dewlap, and hoisted his enormous bulk out of his chair. Clearing his throat and banging his gavel on the rostrum, he shouted, "Gentlemen, the meeting will come to order!"

Gentlemen? Well, maybe it was force of habit.

Ryder banged his gavel again. "Gentlemen!" he shouted, "I'd like to start the meeting by commending the wonderful combined efforts of the central labor union councils of Minneapolis in the construction of this beautiful new building!" The crowd roared its approval.

The old Labor Temple down the street stood empty and was scheduled to fall to the wrecking ball. I had been in the building a few times, since it had sometimes been rented out for concerts. The main hall was three stories high, with a gallery at the back and a hippodrome-style roof that was covered with frescoes. The roof was held up by enormous, thick pillars. It was a wonderful old building, reminiscent of a cathedral.

How could the laborites abandon it in favor of the ugly brick-and-glass box in which we had gathered? The new temple, which was no temple, was devoid of character. The uninspired modern decor in the downstairs bar included, among other abominations, a plastic rubber tree and a stuffed fish. Tradition was not a priority in the labor movement anymore.

Ryder banged his gavel again, bringing the celebration to an end. "Gentlemen!" he yelled. "And ladies!" he amended, smiling. "The next order of business is the swearing-in of new members!"

And so we were sworn in, each of us mumbling promises to support our union brothers and the national pipefitters' union. A polite round of applause followed the ceremony. There was no booing.

When the meeting adjourned, Ryder made a point of inviting all of us "gals" to join him and the boys at the bar to celebrate. Apparently, adjourning to the bar was the time-honored tradition that would, or could, never be abandoned. None of us felt we could refuse.

I ordered a 7-Up and straddled a stool. "We did it," I said, clinking my glass on Sonny's. "We are now official union people. Poor Mom."

Behind us, Ryder yelled, "To the ladies!"

A roar of drunken approval followed his toast, and Sonny, Lila, Pam, and I raised our glasses. The drinking had obviously started well before the meeting. I saw faces that I knew had not made it upstairs for the swearing-in, or for any of the other union business. Many of them seemed eager for the new inductees to catch up with them. Several unidentifiable drinks appeared on the bar in front of us.

The bartender had a thick yellow ponytail and a pudgy pink face. His smile had about as much sincerity as the Cheshire Cat's. "Congratulations to the first lady gasmen!" he said, wiping water rings and spilled beer from the polished oak bar, which from the look of it had been salvaged from the old Labor Temple.

"Tell me," the bartender said, leaning into Sonny. "Can a guy still get a job at Minnegasco?"

"Why?" she shot back. "You getting tired of wiping countertops for a living?"

"No-o-o. I just love gals with green eyes and sharp tongues, is all. Besides, I can get a job there any time I want to, honey, thanks to *him*." He nodded in Ryder's direction. "I just don't want to. Unless you want me to."

Sonny and I turned our backs to the bartender and our

faces to the Local 340 crowd. Our union brothers were celebrating mightily, slapping each other's backs and running up bar tabs. It looked as though the monthly meetings were mainly a pretext to drink. I saw JE in a corner by himself. He finished his drink and ducked out the side door.

Sipping 7-Up, I watched as Box made his way through the crowd and stopped in front of Sonny and me.

"I'd like to buy the new union members a drink," he said. "Proud ta work with ya." He looked at our glasses. "What'll ya have?"

"Windsor and Seven," Sonny said. I started to protest, but she whispered that this was Box, and protocol mandated that we let him buy a round.

A tenth-grade disaster when I had guzzled Budweiser as if it were Kool-Aid had turned me from drink. Consequently, I always had to explain that I was *not* a member of AA. I just didn't like the stuff.

Untouched drinks were lined up behind me on the bar. I looked at Box. "No thank you," I said. "I don't drink."

"You're not an AA'er, are you?" he asked, concerned.

"No, I . . ."

"Good! Here, hold on. I'll order you a *great* drink." In the deafening racket of the bar my protests went unheard.

Box ordered me something and told me it tasted just like a chocolate malt. He was right. It *did* taste like a chocolate malt. I knocked it back in a flash, and someone ordered another one. Then two more appeared. And disappeared. I swiped at the Brazil nuts stuck in the bottoms of the stubby glasses, fished them out, and ate them. Everyone

seemed warm and friendly. All these people buying chocolate malts—*for me!*

I looked over at Sonny. To my vast surprise, she didn't
seem warm and friendly. She wasn't smiling like everyone
else. "What happened to that drink that was there a minute ago?" she demanded.

"Drink?"

"That Smith and Currans," she said. "Urbin just bought
it for you."

"Urbin?"

"Can ya give me a two-word answer?" She put her face
closer to mine. "You're smashed!"

"No," I said, with much deliberation. "I do not drink."

"Those Smith and Currans, my dear, are full of booze.
You've been slugging them down like they were made out
of water."

"Not water! Chocolate malts! Only they're a little run-
nier. Runny, runny, runny, runny."

Sonny rolled her eyes in exasperation.

"'Nother Smirnoff and Burrins, pla-leez," I slurred, sliding off my stool.

"Come on," Sonny said. "We're going home."

The last thing I remembered seeing was Urbin's head. It
was stuck in the window of Sonny's rusted-out station
wagon, asking her if she needed any help. I thought it was
sweet of him to ask.

The next day, I awoke with a relentlessly pounding head.
I stumbled into the bathroom, found an old bottle of as-

pirin, and managed to snap off the cap. I swallowed a couple and then barfed. I crawled back to my couch, praying for God's forgiveness.

Sonny was across the room, watching me. She made no effort to help me. When I landed on my stomach, arms and legs dangling over the sides of the couch, she finally spoke.

"You don't look so hot," she said.

"Ugh."

"Lenny called. He wanted to know if you made it home in one piece." As a supervisor, Lenny wasn't a union member and did not attend union meetings. So my misfortune was public knowledge.

I opened one eye. Sonny was sitting in my favorite over-stuffed chair, her feet crossed on the ottoman. She held a coffee mug in one hand and ran fingers through her hair with the other. Her hair was wet. She had obviously spent the night, and she had had time to shower and make coffee before I awoke. I wondered how much of the day I had lost, and what day it was. I sure didn't want to hear about my boss calling.

"What time is it?"

"Noon."

"Day?"

"Thursday."

"Whew!"

"Relax. 'Course you look like you've managed that already." She sipped coffee. Watching her made my head swim. "We aren't expected till tomorrow."

She must have told Lenny everything. Benedict Arnold, I thought. If I didn't die first, he would fire me. One false move, one juvenile act, one bad judgment, and I get canned two minutes after making probation. Talk about bad luck.

"Urbin called, too," Sonny said. "To apologize for buying you a drink."

"Please don't run me a list of all the callers," I begged.

"Yah."

"I don't drink," I whispered.

"That's what you kept telling everybody last night. Either they believed you and had fun watching you make a fool of yourself, or they didn't and figured you for an alkie." She got up and went into my kitchen. She returned in a little while, carrying a tray with toast and tomato juice.

"Eat this," she said, shoving the tray under my nose. "It might make you feel better. Then again, it might not."

I put a corner of toast in my mouth and started to chew. Eventually I was able to sit halfway upright, propping my face in my fists. My head weighed a hundred pounds, even though it had to be empty. I thanked Sonny for her discretion and complimented her on her choice of the navy cords and cable-knit sweater from my wardrobe. She made my clothes look good.

"I guess I really screwed up," I said, needing more toast and thankful that she hadn't buttered it.

"Don't worry. Your little fiasco will go down as just another one of those things that guys can do better than girls—namely, drink."

"Don't say *drink*."

"Yup," she went on, mercilessly. "I think you're going to be remembered forever as that colored girl who likes them Smirnoff and Burrins!"

# 11

## Pink Performance

ON FRIDAY, LENNY ASKED to see Sonny and me in his office after the work orders had been handed out. He left me with no time to plan an acceptable line of defense for my unacceptable behavior. I decided simply to ask for his lenience and forgiveness. After all, Lenny was an Elmo, not a Rockhead. I could reason with him, I hoped.

Sonny followed me down the stairs from the shop to Lenny's cubbyhole, which was crammed with spools of blueprints in round cardboard tubs. All of Minnegasco seemed to be in need of repair, and it was Lenny's job to oversee the work. From the looks of the place, it was a wonder that anything got done.

The master engineer and department head, Sidney Wimple, was housed in the office next to Lenny's. Wimple had twice as much space as Lenny, and ten times the mess. Their cubicles were separated by partitions. No privacy here, I thought. Just as well Wimple hadn't gotten to work yet. Maybe he'd never be told about my first union meeting.

Wimple had strung up a mostly dead philodendron with one long tendril that stretched across his office and into Lenny's. The plant was stapled to the partitions every three feet or so. It looked like a party decoration somebody had forgotten to take down.

Lenny finally arrived, holding his bottomless mug of coffee. He and his Minnesota Vikings mug were inseparable, even when the mug was empty. I watched in admiration as he skillfully edged his way around the corner of his cluttered desk, avoiding spools of blueprints while he pecked at the rim of his Super Bowl collectible. He sat down in his chair without spilling a drop and invited Sonny and me to get our own coffee before settling in.

Sonny left hurriedly, saying she would get coffee for both of us, and leaving me, the guilty party, alone with my supervisor. I pulled a pack of cigarettes from my shirt pocket, then spotted a sign in the midst of the desk clutter: THANK YOU FOR NOT SMOKING. I put the offending hard pack back in my pocket and tried to relax without the aid of stimulants.

I had no trouble avoiding eye contact with Lenny, since he paid no attention to me. With his chin resting on his chest, he studied a bulging pocket protector in the breast pocket of his short-sleeved white polyester golf shirt. The pocket protector was so full of pens that the surrounding material was pulled out of shape. I could see little holes in the polyester that had resulted from its being stretched to the limit.

Lenny selected a black Bic pen and slid it behind his right ear, already burdened with the bow of his glasses and a hearing aid. Adding the Bic to the mix threw the right side of his head out of balance.

Pen mounted and set—I knew not for what—Lenny frowned at the mess on his desk. He held his mug out, away from potential danger, and dug with one hand through a pile of papers, muttering and swearing as he worked. I was certain that he didn't know I was still there.

Finally, Lenny found two legal-looking documents at the bottom of the pile and carefully slipped them out. Pink! Everybody knows that the infamous pink slip means trouble.

I watched, frozen.

He balanced his mug on a teetering stack of papers. He pulled the pen from behind his ear and signed both pink documents. His paperwork completed, he lifted his eyes and saw me. He blinked in obvious confusion, realizing for the first time that I had not gone with Sonny to get coffee and that I had overheard his swear words. He blushed tomato-red and said, "Excuse my French."

"French is a lovely language," I said.

He chuckled nervously and held one of the pink slips out to me. There was nothing else to do but to take it.

"Thank you," I said reluctantly. So the sentence would be passed on as planned, in spite of my willingness to ignore his French. Not very sporting, I thought.

"Is there something wrong?" he asked anxiously. "You've done very well, you know. I'm real proud of both you girls, er, women." He sipped his coffee and looked at me through his wire-rimmed glasses.

Done well? Proud of us? For what? Getting drunk? This didn't make sense. But Lenny was never sarcastic.

I looked down at the pink document—and noticed, for the first time, the words PERFORMANCE EVALUATION emblazoned across the top. *Performance* evaluation? I *wasn't* getting fired? And we'd done *well*? And Lenny was *proud* of us?

Self-absorption and self-pity had made me blind. I knew a performance evaluation was coming. We had been told to expect one immediately following induction into the union, and I had forgotten. Thank heavens, I thought, watching Lenny concentrate on his coffee mug. It was all I could do to keep from telling him how relieved I was.

Seeing me brighten up, he said, "Take a moment to read it while I go get more coffee. When I come back, I'll answer questions, if you have any." He left in a rush, presumably because his mug was empty. Sonny came in and got her report. Squeezed in among the blueprints in Lenny's office, Sonny and I sat reading silently.

The one-page report listed basic elements of job performance and scored an employee's work from one to four. According to the report, I'd apparently been a boring worker:

| | |
|---|---|
| Arrives at work on time | 3 |
| Is presentable and prepared to work | 3 |
| Is knowledgeable about his assignments | 3 |
| Completes projects on time | 3 |

And so forth. Adequate. Consistently above average. No
failures but no shining performances.

I peeked at Sonny's performance report, which was supposed to be private. She'd gotten all threes, too. I nudged
her and held up my report for her to see. Squinting, she
gave me a sidelong look and snorted.

Lenny returned, mug first, and maneuvered around his
desk. He slurped happily, his eyes inviting comment.

"There isn't much variety in these grades," Sonny
started.

Lenny sipped methodically. He didn't seem to be in any
hurry to respond. "We don't think of them as grades," he finally said, draining his coffee. He looked at his mug and
frowned. Fran Tarkenton frowned back.

"Ah-huh. Well, how is it that we both got all threes?"
Sonny asked, picking up my report and holding it up for
Lenny to see, as if he didn't already know.

I was wondering the same thing, but since I was still reveling in not being fired, I sat quietly, grinning. Though it
*was* hard to believe that we had performed exactly the
same in every way. A case in point: I had never come to

work late. On the other hand, I couldn't think of a day when Sonny arrived on time. Yet there, next to "Arrives at work on time," Sonny's report showed a three. Just like mine.

I also wondered why it was that we were being evaluated together. Performance reports were usually confidential. But I supposed that it wasn't completely surprising—Lenny, like most of the men, tended to think of Sonny and me as a single unit. It was never just Peggie, or just Sonny. It was Sonny and Peggie. Or *da girls,* or *da women,* or *da ladies.* We were not really individuals.

On the other hand, honesty forced me to consider whether I really wanted to be evaluated apart from Sonny. We shared similar views on everything from politics to education to social policy. We had become close friends quickly. I was immensely grateful to Lenny for recognizing right away that we might need each other's support, and for teaming us together as often as he could.

"This loose measure, and I emphasize the word *loose,*" began Lenny, "is only an estimate of . . ."

"Yes," Sonny cut him off. "But why bother with looseness? These aren't accurate. I want my record to reflect absolute fact, not looseness. These aren't the truth!"

"As I see it, they are," Lenny said calmly.

"How could we have improved on that stop sign we put up at South Yard?" Sonny demanded.

Lenny shrugged. "I don't think you could have."

"Painting at Linden?"

"Not much to improve on there."

"Fact is, we've gone out of our way to be perfect, because we've *had* to be!"

"And you've been very successful at it, too," he said, without a trace of condescension. His manner was positive and pleasant but firm. "But I like to leave room for improvement."

Sonny cocked her head, relaxed, and smiled. She didn't really care about "looseness." She just wanted to be certain that Lenny appreciated the effort that we had put into our projects. Lenny, on the other hand, was making it clear that he *was* aware of it. Both had made their respective points, and both now seemed satisfied.

"These don't go into your permanent files," Lenny said. "I do these more or less to give you an idea of how I view your work. I think you should be extremely satisfied. I am."

"So am I," I said, thinking how I'd come in twenty minutes ago expecting to be fired. It was nice to be talking about above-average performance and not about Wednesday night's performance.

Lenny nodded in my direction. "Peggie," he asked, "do you have anything that you want to talk about? Or any questions?"

"Well, there is one thing," I said, feeling the kind of high I'd always felt after leaving the confessional. "Do the men get *blue* evaluations?"

Sonny laughed and spilled her coffee all over herself and Lenny's paperwork and me.

"I would have expected that question from *her*, not from

*you*," Lenny said, grinning at both of us. "I know it isn't always easy for you two, being girls . . ."

"Being a girl isn't hard at all," Sonny butted in.

"I mean being a girl and having the guts to work here. So congratulations. I'm really glad you made probation and got into the union." Lenny raised his empty mug in a toast. "Sometimes it's hard to know if it's okay to complain about working conditions, but please don't think you can't tell me if something's wrong. My door is open, and what you say to me in confidence will stay that way."

Sonny and I looked at each other. We were union members, so theoretically we were protected. I liked Lenny, but he was still a man, in a man's environment. Could we really speak freely? If I were told him about JE, what would he do? What *could* he do? What did I *want* him to do? Lenny waited patiently, as if he expected us to complain.

"There is one person," I said carefully. "A foreman. Rockhead. We would rather not work with him."

"It isn't just that Rockhead makes racist and sexist comments all day long," Sonny began.

"All day long," I emphasized.

"But Rockhead is so stupid he actually thinks we agree with him when he says things like how women really want to stay home to watch kids and do ladies' work, and how we, me and Peggie, are taking jobs from men so we should get married fast, and how Indians are drunks, and Mexicans are lazy, and Chinks are real smart but funny-looking. The guy makes my head spin!"

"I'm not surprised," Lenny said.

We stared at Lenny. "You know about him?"

"I didn't for sure. But I suspected. He's been saying that stuff around us for years. I wondered if he'd have the nerve to say it around you. No, I'm not surprised," Lenny concluded. "He's not a real subtle guy."

"No kidding," Sonny said.

"I'll try not to send you with him. But he's a foreman. And foremen work with crews, so I can't promise you that you'll never work with him again. I will talk to him, though. Today. It might do him some good. I'll tell him to keep his mouth shut around you, and if he does, I guess that's the best we can expect. You need to remember something, though. We're not here to change his horse-poop opinions. We're here to make a living. So what he says on his own time is his own business, and I'm not gonna try to change that, unless he says something that affects you personally. Fair enough?"

"We'll see," Sonny said.

Suddenly, Lenny leaned forward conspiratorially. "Just so you know," he said, "your favorite foreman hasn't won any popularity contests with anybody around here for as long as I've known him. I think he figured he could go after you two so he could rub some of the poop off himself. From what I hear, though, it's not working. If it's any help, having him against you seems to be doing you some good with the other guys."

Sonny and I looked at each other. This was news.

"Is that it?" he asked.

Sonny looked at me quizzically. I didn't understand why it was easy for me to tell Lenny about Rockhead's behavior, while I was terrified to confide in him about JE. Sonny seemed to understand. She kept my secret.

Lenny peered over the mound of paper on his desk and tapped a finger on his forehead. "Now what else do I need to do?" he asked himself. "Oh, yeah. What one thing can we do here to make the environment for you girls—women—friendlier?"

"That's easy," I said, bringing our meeting to a close. "Hire more women."

# 12

## Just Like One of the Family

MOM AND I were in the habit of calling each other every day. This ritual had begun as a friendly practice when I had first moved away from home. It had become less friendly as I continued to refuse to leave Minnegasco and concentrate one hundred percent on getting a degree in journalism.

"How did your day go?" I asked her, before she had a chance to ask about mine.

"Great!" she said excitedly. "This afternoon I spoke to a woman about a domestic-servant story I'm working on. A Mrs. James Lily from Stillwater. Mrs. Lily said she'd love to let me interview her."

"What's the big deal?" I asked, confused. Mom knew as well as any reporter that people liked to see their names in print, even at the risk of being misquoted—which of course they always thought they were when things didn't work out right.

"Mrs. James Lily has a live-in maid." I could hear Mom take a sip of coffee. I waited. There had to be more scratch to this story. "The maid," Mom continued in her quiet voice, "is just like one of the family." This last was said in a distinct Southern drawl.

"Don't tell me," I said. "This maid, whose name is probably Mammy, jus' loves her li'l ole chilluns half to death."

"Well, Mrs. Lily didn't say what her maid's name was, or whom she did or did not love. But she did tell me it was terribly difficult to get good colored help up here."

Mom loved dealing with this kind of thing. It made for good copy. We both knew that Mrs. James Lily suffered from the common delusion that all black people are alike, are interchangeable, and have lives that don't count. It wasn't the first time that Mom had been mistaken for a white person over the phone. Some of her best journalistic scoops had started out just like this one. Mom's pronunciation was plain Richfield, Minnesota, by way of Iowa, but her manner of speech was redolent of good books and a college education. She was an amateur etymologist and a relentless grammarian. People sometimes didn't realize to whom they were speaking.

"Exactly how hard is it to get good colored help these days?" I asked.

"Well," Mom giggled, "Mrs. Lily said wasn't it just too bad about that dumb equal rights thing. All the colored boys takin' up white jobs. Colored girls wantin' to stay at home."

"Imagine that," I said.

"So you see of course there is a problem. If all the colored gals stay at home, who'll do the laundry for Mrs. Lily?"

"The Irish?" I guessed.

When we stopped laughing, Mom finished telling her story. "Mrs. James Lily would like to continue our delightful conversation. In her home. Over tea!"

"Poor Mrs. Lily," I said, seeing how she had let Mom's sweet demeanor lure her into a deadly trap. "Can I go with you? I mean, *may* I go with you?" Who wouldn't want to be there when Mrs. Lily set her eyes on Mom? "As an educational experience," I added.

"Absolutely," Mom said. "I would love your company. I'll pick you up on Thursday at 5:30 sharp."

"I'll be ready," I assured her.

On Thursday, I was stuck working with Rockhead, but I hardly noticed as I wondered all day about Mrs. Lily. After work, I rushed home and showered quickly. Deciding what to wear shouldn't have been difficult, but Mom would expect me to make the correct impression. A pile of rejected ensembles grew on my bed. Finally I settled on a navy-and-white pinstriped blouse, dark green corduroys, a wool cardigan, and a camel blazer. I slipped on a pair of loafers and consulted the mirror. *Student,* my reflection said back to me. *Wealthy student.* A specter to confuse Mrs. Lily yet satisfy Mom. I went to the kitchen to make dinner.

Unlike getting dressed, creating dinner presented no challenges. There are only so many things one can do with tuna, and by now I did all of them well. I assembled a sandwich, ate it, and washed it down with a glass of V-8. The dishes were washed in no time. I finished an after-dinner smoke one minute before Mom arrived at my St. Paul apartment.

"You look nice," she said as I climbed into her Volvo. "You know, you appear more intelligent when you lay your blue jeans to rest. Pity you don't do it more often." Ignoring my groan, she continued, "You may borrow my lipstick. You'll find it in my purse. Top-left pocket."

I put the stuff on my lips. It was easier than arguing, since she won all these little battles.

"I'll introduce you as my daughter, who is studying journalism . . ."

"That's mighty white of you," I interrupted.

"Of course you're studying journalism, dear," Mom said slowly, articulating each word with forced sweetness. "I am trying to say, without condescending, that there is simply no reason to mention NSP."

"That's okay," I replied, folding my arms across my chest. "Because I fit pipe at Minnegasco. I'll tell her that."

"No," she said, using her mother-has-spoken voice. "I'm introducing you as a student. We don't want to give a wrong impression."

"Wrong impression?" I nearly shouted. "If you tell her only that I'm a student, and that I don't have a job, you *will* be giving a wrong impression. Where are your professional ethics?"

"Where is *your* pride? Tonight, you're a student," she commanded. "And that's that."

We drove straight east, past downtown St. Paul and through a tangle of suburbs near the St. Croix River. We were lost in a plush neighborhood of large houses on curved roads, all of which seemed to have Hillcrest in their names. We finally found Hillcrest Circle.

The Lily driveway was long and winding, and the Lily house was hidden from the road by a grove of mature oak trees. The design was probably meant to discourage the uninvited, and even though we were invited, I didn't feel welcome. I scanned the grounds, looking for the pack of thick-chested Dobermans I expected to be there protecting the Lilys from folks like us. But all was quiet, in a moneyed sort of way.

As we expected, the Lily house was a mansion. Mom rang the doorbell, and far away inside we could hear chimes sounding. After a long wait, the polished-oak door was swung open by the blackest person I had ever seen. Her color was set off by her starched white uniform. She glared past us at an unidentifiable spot somewhere on the lawn and inquired how she might help us.

"Mary Jane Saunders, from the *Pioneer Press*," Mom said. "We're expected."

That was only partially true, of course. I doubted very much that *we* were expected. I was suddenly embarrassed and feeling guilty for being involved in a journalistic joke that might ultimately be played out at the expense of the woman who stood before us. We had been so eager to have fun with Mrs. Lily that we hadn't considered the possible repercussions on the maid.

Of course it was too late to worry about that. So I followed my mother and the black-and-white woman through a high-ceilinged foyer with golden oak wainscoting and mauve wallpaper. The foyer felt a good deal friendlier than the adjacent sitting room, where we were asked to wait.

The sitting room was white. Refrigerator white. The walls, the shag carpeting, even the baby grand piano were all white. An orange floral arrangement on the white mantelpiece added a single splash of color.

Mom and I were instructed to settle into white leather chairs. Madam would join us shortly. The white leather sucked us into our seats like a vacuum. We waited in silence. The Lily sitting room did not invite conversation.

In time, a large woman in a flowing gown swept into the room, arms extended and apologies on her lips for having made us wait. Mom and I struggled out of the leather. "So sorry," Mrs. Lily said, glancing down at Mom and finally seeing her. "I was expecting a reporter. I am not hiring any help right now. Try closer to Christmas. We're always busier around here at Christmas."

"Mary Jane Saunders from the *Pioneer Press*," Mom said,

extending a hand. She was several inches shorter than Mrs. Lily and was wearing a fitted business suit. Mrs. Lily spun slightly on her heels and stepped back, as if to get a better look at this person who said she was a reporter. Her gown swished and rustled, looking silly next to Mom's sensible day-wear.

Mrs. Lily must have been thinking the same thing, because she yanked at the skirt of her swaying dress as if it were a naughty puppy on a leash. "I'm afraid I don't understand," she drawled. "I thought you were looking for domestic work."

"No," Mom said. "I'm here to do an interview *about* domestics."

Realizing her gaffe, Mrs. Lily sank into one of her leather chairs, looking as pale as her decor. Mom sat. The furniture hissed as she settled into it. The ambience of the Lily sitting room made me feel like an extra in a Fred Astaire movie from the 1930s. Only nobody was dancing. Mrs. Lily spotted me at last, and narrowed her eyes.

"Oh," Mom said. "This is my daughter Margaret. She is a journalism student at the University of Minnesota." *Communications student,* I corrected her silently. I gave Mrs. Lily a full frontal view of all my teeth, thinking that a big smile might help her to relax and regain her color.

"I assumed Margaret would be welcome to observe the interview process. I hope that I did not assume incorrectly?" Mom locked eyes with our hostess.

"No. I mean, yes. Oh, dear." Mrs. Lily smiled weakly.

"Certainly. She's . . . your daughter is certainly welcome." Looking uncomfortable, Mrs. Lily called, "Morgan!"

"I am also employed as a pipefitter trainee at Minnegasco, in Minneapolis," I blurted.

Mom shuddered visibly but recovered quickly, as was her style. "Margaret is the first female pipefitter ever to work there," she said, her nostrils flaring.

Mrs. Lily narrowed her eyes again. "I didn't know girls could be pipefitters."

"Women," I corrected her. "It's all very new." I was enjoying watching Mrs. Lily squirm. Vindictiveness is never sporting, but at that moment it felt so good. I could almost taste her anxiety, so I set aside any feelings of guilt for later consideration.

Mrs. Lily looked from me to Mom and from Mom to me. "Morgan!" she called again.

Morgan appeared, black and white. She stood nearly at attention. *Just like one of the family*, I thought.

"Morgan, bring some tea for our guests." Mrs. Lily didn't look at Morgan, and there was a tinge of fear in her voice. I thought I saw a trace of satisfaction pass across Morgan's face. Then it was gone. "Please," added Mrs. Lily, as an afterthought.

Mrs. Lily didn't see me roll my eyes. Morgan did. I wished that I could penetrate her masklike impassivity and wondered what humiliations she had suffered in the Lily household. Mom was interviewing the wrong person, I thought.

Mrs. Lily shook her bottle-white head and forced her hands to relax in her lap. Regaining a little of her poise, she asked, "Miss *Sanders*, is it?"

"Right," Mom said, not bothering to correct her. "Is Morgan your maid's first name or her last name?"

"Morgan? Oh, yes. I'm sorry. Let me think. Jane is her first name, I believe. Morgan is her last name." Mrs. Lily rubbed her temples and took the plunge. "I hope that you didn't take what I said on the phone the other day personally?"

"Right," Mom said. "How long has Ms. Morgan been with you?"

"I'm sorry. Been with us?" Mrs. Lily stared at the ceiling a moment. "I think it's been six or seven years. I don't re-member exactly. I really didn't mean it the other day, you know."

Mom flipped a page in her notebook. "You said on the phone that Ms. Morgan is, and I quote, 'Just like one of the family.' Would you please explain what you meant by that statement?"

"Oh, dear, I'm sorry. Did I say that?"

"Yes."

"Well, she's . . . she's such a darling," Mrs. Lily said, and chuckled nervously. Mom and I didn't laugh. "We . . . we love her so. We just wouldn't know what to do without our darling."

Mom waited.

"On the phone the other day, I didn't mean to imply that

Jane—I mean Morgan—oh dear, I'm afraid I'm not making much sense, am I?"

"Could you give me an example of how Ms. Morgan is included in your family? For instance, where does she eat her meals, with you or elsewhere?"

"Well," Mrs. Lily said, warily, "she *serves* our meals."

"Then she really isn't like one of the family, is she?" Mom didn't wait for an answer. She flipped another page. "What are Ms. Morgan's other duties, besides serving your meals? Laundry? Housecleaning? Child care?" Mom studied her notebook and waited.

"All of those," Mrs. Lily said, thrusting her chin forward. "But I insist that the children make their own beds."

"Right. Does Ms. Morgan go on vacations with you and your family?"

"Yes."

"When does she vacation on her own?"

"I'm sorry, could you repeat that question?"

"Is Ms. Morgan allowed time off, for instance, to visit her own family? Does she get her own vacation time?"

"Why, of course." Mrs. Lily seemed surprised by the question. "She has every other Sunday off."

Mom stared at Mrs. Lily for a moment. "What are Ms. Morgan's wages?" she asked.

Just then, Jane Morgan returned, carrying a large tray laden with a fancy porcelain teapot and matching cups and saucers. She carefully set the tray down on a glass-and-chrome coffee table, turned her back on Mrs. Lily, and winked at Mom and me. Bravo, I thought. She must have delayed serving the tea so that she could eavesdrop.

Mrs. Lily's apologies grew more numerous, until they finally took over the interview. Mom kept trying, but the only thing she could get from Mrs. Lily was apologies—lots of apologies. Mom took a final sip of tea and snapped her notebook shut. Frustration seemed to propel her as she bounced out of the clinging chair, thanked our hostess, and hastily prepared to leave. I was still enjoying myself and couldn't understand why she was in such a hurry to go.

Outside, I said, "I haven't had so much fun since Sonny threw the underwear at the guys in the Linden Building. Nice going, Mom."

"Mmm."

"Do you think those people ever let Jane Morgan talk? Just like one of the family! Think she got any fun out of our visit? I hope so. It would help to justify all those nasty primal feelings I've had in the past hour."

"Perhaps," Mom said.

I looked at her with concern. "Is something wrong?"

"You said you enjoyed yourself."

"You bet I did. Thanks for letting me come."

"You could be doing the same thing," she said quietly. "On a permanent basis. You would do it extremely well."

Poor Mrs. Lily. And poor dumb Peggie. Mom had gotten both of us in the same trip.

"It wasn't *that* much fun," I lied.

# 13

## Safety First

SONNY AND I SETTLED into the Buildings and Grounds routine: painting, yard work, pipefitting, defending our right to be there, and attending a monthly safety meeting. Safety on the job was the single thing on the agenda at these meetings. It was a good thing, because one more subject would have been two subjects too many.

For one particularly difficult meeting, Lenny found a film on ladder safety starring the twin of the bouffanted woman in the hoop skirt who had taught us how to stop, drop, and roll under our grade school desks in the event of nuclear attack. As a woman, I found the film fascinating.

It's not easy to demonstrate safe use of a ladder when you're dressed in a hoopskirt. I wondered how many takes had been necessary, and how many bumps and bruises the hoopskirted lady had gotten while she was making the film.

When the film ended, it spun off the reel. Lenny retrieved it, wound it up, and then stared out over his comatose audience.

"Ah, well, that was interesting," he said. "Anyone have a question?"

There were no questions.

"Any comments on what we've just seen?"

There were no comments.

"Don," Lenny addressed the garbage truck driver. "What did you think about never stepping on the top two rungs of a stepladder? Sound like a safe idea to you?"

Don blinked. "Rungs?"

For fifteen minutes, as specified in his supervisor's handbook, Lenny worked his audience. Then he dismissed us. Someone kicked Box awake. He stood, zombielike, walked straight outside, and stood in the snow.

The matter of safety did not end with monthly meetings. As a way of saying thank you to departments with allegedly good safety records, the company threw "safety dinners." Judging from the regularity of these dinners, any number of accidents per department seemed to qualify. Even though we were sometimes referred to as Bungles and Goofs, Buildings and Grounds usually did have an excellent safety record. And so we were awarded a dinner.

As the gala event neared, I was repeatedly asked the same question. "You're coming to the safety dinner, aren'tcha?"

*You must be kidding,* I thought.

"Dinner's free! Steak's free, too!"

Shrugging noncommittally, I would answer, "We'll see." *I'll go when the pope ain't Italian,* I thought.

Several days before the dinner, I stood on the loading dock at the Northeast Yard with Elmo. We were moving all the Minnegasco appliance stores to new locations. We shifted stock around from the stores in Southdale, Brookdale, and Ridgedale until each new location was ready to have its stock returned. I was sick of shopping malls. The work required nothing from my mind, but it drained my body and left me with just enough energy to crawl home at the end of the workday. At sixty-something, Elmo went home looking as if he'd spent the day fishing and hadn't lifted anything heavier than his pole. It wasn't fair.

We had leveled the power tailgate of our truck as close as we could to the dock and were about to hike a washing machine out of it when I spotted Lenny making his careful-not-to-spill-his-coffee way toward us. I set my end of the machine down and Elmo, following my glance, set his end down, too.

"Well, I see you two are making good progress," Lenny said from behind his Vikings collectible.

"Yah," Elmo said, nodding. He had removed his engineer cap, and the two men stared at the washer as if they expected it to dance a jig. "She's goin' real good," he continued. I smiled at this compliment, but then I remembered that "she" was the job, not I. "Dis one here, she's a good worker, too," Elmo said, pointing his crumpled cap at me. Both their heads nodded up and down, neither taking his eyes from the washing machine.

They were cute, I thought, knowing how much they would have hated that assessment. But they *were* cute, in a homely way.

Lenny turned to me. "Are you going to the safety dinner? I didn't see your name on the sign-up sheet, or Sonny's either. The sign-up's on the union meeting bulletin board over in the carpenter shop."

"Ya better get some steak," Elmo said. "Fatten ya up a little. Get ya some muscles."

"I don't eat steak," I said.

Lenny wrinkled his nose. Elmo scratched his head.

"Don't eat steak?" Elmo said suspiciously.

"No," I said, conscious of their wide-eyed disapproval. "I don't care for it."

"T'ain't American," Elmo said, shaking his head.

Lenny said, "You know, I think they serve lobster. Yeah, and chicken, maybe. I mean, if you really don't want steak."

He smiled the kindest blue-eyed smile. I wished Sonny had been with me. I needed her strength and fast thinking to get us out of this safety dinner stuff. These two made me want to make cute little muffin-man cookies with their names, Lenny and Elmo, printed in chocolate across their chests. The kind I used to make for my brothers, Bobby, Frank, and Christopher, until they were too old to appreciate them.

"I like lobster and chicken," I said, feeling the need to please them.

"I'm glada dat," Elmo said, hitching up his pants. "I t'ought maybe you was one a dem veggietarians or somethin'."

"I'll get Sid to put you both down for lobster, then?" Lenny asked happily.

"Well, we . . ." I stalled. Why couldn't I just tell them that Sonny and I had no intention of going to the safety dinner, and that our decision was final? If only Elmo's white hair had been tucked neatly under his engineer cap, instead of standing up in a halo of static. If only Lenny wasn't wearing those high-water polyester pants with white socks and shiny black shoes. If only they hadn't been standing there smiling with puppy-dog eyes, looking as if they'd be hurt if I refused. They were pushing all my maternal caretaker buttons.

"I don't know, Lenny. I need to talk to Sonny first."

"Ah, well, I sure hope you girls come 'cause . . . well, 'cause we all want you there, that's why."

I wondered if Rockhead wanted us there. He probably did. That way, he'd be guaranteed an audience for his girl-bashing. Would JE be there? Probably.

"We talked, of course," I said slowly. "But we had sort of decided not to go." I didn't mention that Sonny and I had fallen into hysterics at the ridiculous suggestion that we should attend a safety dinner.

"Oh," Lenny said, crestfallen. "I was really hoping that you would grace us with your presence." Where was this kind of talk coming from? "I sure wish you'd reconsider.

Fact is, this would mark the first time . . ."—he turned bright red—"that attractive women . . ."—redder—"ever came to a B&G safety dinner." Redder still. "Please?"

He had me. "Okay," I said. The snake.

Sonny and I were the first females to attend a B&G safety dinner. Which raised several questions. How should we dress? The dinner was to be held at Nye's Polonaise Room, a family restaurant in Northeast Minneapolis that required a clean shirt and, possibly, a sport coat. But what did this mean for me? Would I be expected to wear a dress?

"We oughta do this thing up right," Sonny suggested, rocking in the black wicker rocker in my living room. "You know, show 'em we got legs."

"I think they know we have legs," I said.

"You know what I mean. Don't pretend you don't."

"Yeah, but you really *do* have legs."

"And you don't?" Sonny wagged a finger at me and shook her head in frustration. Her yellow braids flew around her head and hit her in the face as she spoke. She looked like a stubborn little Dutch girl.

I knew where the discussion was heading, and I didn't like it. I always felt uncomfortable talking about my appearance. I had been brought up to believe that self-absorption with what you have no control over is narcissistic. For most of my life, the media, books, cosmetic companies, and a host of others made it clear that to them, an attractive black female was a contradiction in terms. Of course, that was foolish. People who pushed such ideas were blind. I didn't like it. But I also didn't care to discuss my supposed beauty.

I thought it was odd that suddenly, in the late 1960s, black became beautiful and desirable. The enthusiastic way in which people, and especially white people, jumped on this new black-is-beautiful bandwagon seemed too good to be true. Something about this new attitude reminded me of bell-bottom pants. How long would it be before it went out of style?

"You don't pay attention to yourself," Sonny said. "You're pretty!"

"Yes, and so are all politicians' wives," I said, irrelevantly. "You want a tuna sandwich?"

Sonny followed me into my kitchen, where there were no dirty dishes in the sink, no trash in the trash bin, and no meat thawing on the counter.

"Sandwich sounds good," she said, taking a visual inventory of the hospital-spotless kitchen with critical eyes. "I noticed when I stayed here before that you've got a lot of tuna."

"Yeah."

"I also noticed that you don't have anything else."

"Yeah."

"What's the deal? Are you afraid to cook? Or afraid of cows and birds and pigs?"

"Yeah."

"Yeah, what?"

"Yeah, both, kind of," I said. "I hate to cook. I also don't like red meat. And I hate to clean up a bunch of dirty dishes, especially after I've just had a good meal. The thought of all those greasy dishes makes me nervous and kills my appetite." I sliced a piece of bread. "You see, a tuna sandwich requires one spoon for the mayo and one knife for spreading the tuna on the bread," I said, handing her a sandwich on a paper plate.

Sonny scoffed. "I don't suppose you've got a pickle? I know there's no milk. I checked."

"No pickles. No milk either. I can't drink milk. Would you care for a glass of juice?" I asked, like a seasoned hostess.

"Juice? You mean juice in a juice glass? The kind you've got to wash?"

"I don't like to drink out of anything except glass glasses," I said. "I don't have any paper or plastic glasses. Do you want the juice or not?"

Sonny didn't answer right away. She had another question. "What if a friend brings her toddler over here to visit, and the baby wants something to drink? Do you give your glass glasses to two-year-olds?"

"Why not? Children need to learn sooner or later how to drink properly. My house is as good a place as any to learn, I should think."

A grin worked its way across Sonny's face. "Okay, but what if the kid dropped the glass and broke it, and made a big nasty mess?"

"I'd ring for the main-floor maid. She's good. Her name is Peggie."

"Do you wash your glass glasses, or are they disposable?" Sonny asked, grinning like a devil on a mission.

"Juice," I said, ignoring the question. "Do you want it or not?"

"I'll have some, but I think you're strange. I think maybe it comes from being locked up in that girls' school with those nuns. Now look at you. Now you're surrounded by guys. You went from nuns to these seriously guy-type guys. These changes must be playing on your brain in a bad way. There's no other way to explain it." She stared at the tuna sandwich that she needed both hands to hold together and shook her head again.

I set my plate down and slouched across from her at the table. We ate in silence for a while, enjoying the simple food.

Sonny might have turned out to be a person I would have befriended because I worked with her, but not necessarily because I liked her. As I watched her, I knew how grateful I was that she was exactly who she was, and not anybody else. She was the person I wanted and needed beside me at Minnegasco. She had the chutzpah I didn't have. She said the things I could only think. I envied her freedom and honesty. I loved her.

"Peggie," she said, breaking into my thoughts. "This is really bullshit. After all, we've got money." What was she talking about?

"Shit, just 'cause we ain't never had money doesn't mean we've gotta act like we don't know what to do with it once we've got it. Spending money doesn't require a degree. We deserve the best." She wiped her lips with a paper napkin. "Listen, I'm not taking no for an answer," she said. "Tomorrow, we go shopping for new safety dinner dresses. At Dayton's."

She also was bossy.

# 14

## Plaid, Pastel, and Polka-Dot Polyester

THE NIGHT OF THE SAFETY DINNER, I drove. Sonny and I had decided to hit the beaches together. She emerged from her apartment pulling a coat over a black miniskirt, a cream silk blouse, black stockings, and high heels. It was too late for me to go back home and change out of my modest jean skirt and cotton blouse. As for Sonny, she had real style and courage.

We were the last to arrive at Nye's. I was in no hurry. After the union-hall fiasco, I was wary of this new adventure in Minnegasco socializing.

A waxy-faced kid in a tuxedo escorted us to a private

dining room. He knew exactly who we were, and he announced our arrival as if we were visiting royalty. I might have been paranoid about his knowing us, but I wasn't. I assumed that he had been given an animated and detailed description of both of us.

A quick survey caused me to wonder if we had mistakenly been delivered to a conclave of used-car salesmen. *Polyester!* Polyester jackets. Polyester pants. Polyester ties. Pastel polyester. Plaid, striped, and polka-dot polyester. And white shoes—lots of white shoes. Never had I seen such unbridled bad taste.

"The girls made it!" someone called. "I'm in love!" someone else shouted. "Can we eat now?" a third voice cried.

Lenny stood near the bar, holding a drink and looking as if he wanted to drop through the floor. I spotted Urbin in a corner, sipping a cup of coffee. He looked as singular as Sonny and I did, dressed as he was in his blue Minnegasco uniform. Maybe he didn't own any polyester. Ignoring the comments bestowed upon us, Sonny and I moved across the room to greet him. B&G'ers meanwhile filled the seats around the dining table, and with a raised finger Lenny summoned the headwaiter.

Two sets of cleavage in net stockings appeared and began serving. They had faces, but none of the men noticed.

I felt exasperated, confused, and intimidated all at the same time. Sonny and I caught patches of conversation: comparisons of the four females in the room. It bothered me to know that I was sure to score poorly compared to the flamboyantly dressed waitresses, and of course Sonny. It bothered me all the more that I cared. After all, I fancied myself a feminist. No feminist would condone what was going on at Nye's Polonaise Room.

On the other hand, there were gray areas in the matter of feminism. My position on many issues wasn't as clear as those held by many women, or men. What did feminism require of me? Feminism, and Catholicism before it, tended to make me feel guilty. It was a girl's duty, the nuns had preached, to stand behind her husband and support him in his beliefs and endeavors. It was not her business to have political beliefs that conflicted with those of her husband, or to be a rebel, or to stand out in any way. I was painfully working my way out of these ideas, but old habits died hard.

Sitting there, torn between opposing philosophies, I thought ruefully of something James Thurber said: "Sixty minutes of thinking of any kind is bound to lead to confusion and unhappiness." I smiled, however briefly, as yet another quotation popped into my head: "A conclusion is the place where you got tired of thinking."

The waitresses bustled around the banquet table at a furious pace, parrying and dodging both verbal and physical thrusts. Somehow they managed to evade the lechers while maintaining smiles, balancing trays, and getting our dinners served. I admired their fortitude, and I flushed with embarrassment at the company I kept.

The plate set before me was laden with the largest hunk of meat I had ever seen. Leaning to my right, I whispered in Sonny's ear, "I didn't order steak. Did you?"

"No," she answered, though her plate was the same as mine. Looking up and down the table, I could see that we all apparently had "ordered" the same thing.

"Didn't Lenny give us three choices—lobster, chicken, or steak? He said he'd write in lobster for me," I said irritably.

"Same here," Sonny said. "This is not lobster."

I poked my fork into the oily-looking baked potato on my plate. The salad, such as it was, consisted of a few leaves of limp iceberg lettuce with a tomato wedge dumped on top. The last thing I wanted to do was to kick up a fuss and bring those two waitresses back into the room, so I did my best with the edible part of my dinner. Sonny ate her tomato, bolted a drink, and scooped melted ice cream from a tiny dish.

Lenny, sitting directly across the table from us, asked, "Is something wrong? Are your dinners okay?" He dabbed at a corner of his mouth with a giant napkin.

"We didn't order steaks," Sonny said. "Must have been an oversight. We got somebody else's meals."

"Sid," Lenny said, looking questioningly toward his supervisor. "Didn't you order the lobsters?"

Wimple was sitting across from Lenny and right next to Sonny. He turned his round, bald head and stared at our plates. He stuffed a hunk of steak into his mouth before answering.

"No. I'm absolutely certain there were no lobsters on the list," he said. "Just steak."

Sidney Wimple, more commonly known as the Wimp, Wimpless, Wimp-dick, Wimp-ass, Wimp-shit, and a host of other wimpy names, had perfect recall. I knew this because he had told me so on several occasions, having forgotten that he'd told me so already.

Lenny said carefully, "As I think about it, I'm positive. There were two lobsters on that list. I put them there myself."

Nearby revelers suddenly quieted down in order to hear the resolution of this misunderstanding between the boss and his subordinate.

Sidney had dressed in predictable fashion for this soirée. He pushed out his lower lip and barked, "You're wrong, Lennart. I would have noticed."

Lenny, looking redder than the tomato I'd eaten, stared into my eyes with an expression I'd never seen before. I held his gaze, thinking, *Shouldn't he be making eye contact with Wimple? What's going on here?*

I soon learned. "Peggie," he said to me, "you *saw* me write the two lobsters on the list, didn't you?" His fixed stare was still unfathomable. I'd never seen this side of Lenny. And I'd never seen him actually write the lobsters on the list, either.

This was probably an example of what people meant when they said that Sidney Wimple drove people to behave oddly. I had been warned never to enter into a debate with him. Matched up against his lunatic pomposity, you could not win. As I looked at Lenny, I wondered how much abuse he had taken from Wimple.

Before jumping onto Lenny's playing field, I carefully noted the spectators. If I was going to make a fool of myself and get in trouble with anybody other than Wimple, I wanted to be the first to know. What I saw was a roomful of men looking at their plates and concentrating on their meals. But Elmo, Box, and Urbin were all grinning encouraging grins. I took the plunge.

"Yes, I saw that," I lied. "I remember you told me that I *had* to go to the safety dinner now that my entree choice was engraved in ink. I saw Sonny's, too," I added, "and it said lobster." I leaned over the table, looked past Sonny, and smiled at Sidney. "Sorry," I said sweetly.

Wimple deflated. He stabbed a piece of steak with his fork and pointed it at Sonny. "Well, you girls need beefing up, anyway," he said. "Besides, the company paid good money for these steaks." From my side of the table, I heard a few snickers. Sidney was oblivious to them.

I knew my performance had landed me some good ole boy points. And I was gratified that Lenny had chosen me to be the instrument of his private rebellion. I turned toward Sonny and whispered, "I think I'm ready for dessert now."

Everyone returned to the business of eating and conversation. I thought the evening's entertainment was over, but I couldn't have been more mistaken. Wimple, probably fighting off the effects of his injured manhood, turned to Sonny and said in a stage whisper, "You know, I've been married for thirty years now."

"Congratulations," Sonny said.

"Yep, thirty years. And the wife never had to work."

"Really?" Sonny said, a little too innocently. "Does your maid live with you, then? Or does she just come in a few times a week?"

"Maid? We don't have a maid."

"Well, you said the wife—does she have a name, by the way?—never works. That must mean you've got a maid. Unless your house is always a mess." Sonny flicked her hair back and blew smoke from a freshly lit cigarette.

Sid knew how to handle this. "What I meant was a *real* job. She doesn't have a real job. You know, one that brings home the bacon, like mine." I shook my head. *Careful, Sidney.*

"Uh-huh," Sonny said. "Let me be sure I understand this. Unless you've got a job where you bring home the bacon, you aren't truly working. Is that right?"

"Well, there's women's work, of course," Sid explained happily. "But that doesn't count."

Sonny stubbed her cigarette precisely into an ashtray. I noticed that the conversations around me had died down again—surprisingly, considering the subject and the amount of drinking that had been done. The guys seemed willing to go along with anything that would lead to Sidney Wimple's humiliation. The problem was, I didn't think he was capable of being humiliated.

"Could you explain to me," Sonny said slowly, "how women's work doesn't count?"

Sidney took a second to think. It was more than he usually needed.

"Well, women's work doesn't bring in any money." He said it slowly, so Sonny could understand his meaning. "Besides, it's fun. Of course, why am I telling you that? You know better than I do. All you girls love to cook. Have I mentioned to you that in thirty years of marriage, the wife has never served me the same meal twice?"

# 15

## *Sidney Gets Sensitive*

FRANK SUBER WAS BIG. Not fat, but fleshy and tall. He had lost a lung to an illness, and he wheezed when he moved. Nonetheless, Frank liked to keep several steps ahead of his boss, Sidney Wimple.

Frank ate a clove of garlic and walked a mile every day, for health reasons. He had bad eyesight and tried to compensate for it by wearing several pairs of glasses at the same time. Hooked around his enormous ears was a pair of regular glasses, with flip-up sunglasses attached. He always wore prescription sunglasses perched on top of his head, and he kept several pairs of reading glasses in various breast pockets. Each pair had a different correction.

I asked him one time if his eyewear ever got him confused. "No, it's not a problem," he answered, and he proceeded to demonstrate. By the time he was done, both the regular glasses and the sunglasses were balanced on the end of his nose, while one pair of reading glasses dangled perilously from a shirt pocket and a second was on the floor.

Frank was an engineer, so he needed to be able to see tiny, faded lines on blueprints. I figured that his glasses were as necessary to him as the most expensive engineer's tools. I wondered what state his other tools were in. But he was a good engineer, even though he was responsible for the purchase of Suber's Goober.

Suber's Goober, as B&G'ers came to call it, was a gooey, refrigerator-white synthetic substance that Frank claimed was the be-all and end-all in roof repair.

South Yard's flat roof leaked. A lot. Sonny, Urbin, Randy, and I were on that roof constantly, plugging old holes and trying to anticipate new ones. Suber's Goober was supposed to put an end to the repairs. In reality, we traded a sticky black mess for a sticky white mess, and the leaks sprang eternally.

When Frank learned that I had once lived in South Minneapolis, he asked, "Hey, did you ever go to Brotherson's?"

"No," I said. "What is it?"

"Best butcher in the Twin Cities. What kind of stuff do you like to eat?"

"Mostly tuna."

"Brotherson's has tuna. Fresh tuna. Everything they have is fresh, and their prices are really fair. My wife and I go there every week."

More than anything, Frank liked to talk about his health. There was a lot to talk about, and most of it was bad. I didn't mind, except when he spoke in great detail about his operations.

I liked Frank. He never asked me if I was a women's libber, or a radical, or one of those student protesters. He didn't want to know if I preferred *black* to *Afro-American*. He never asked me why I'd want to work for Minnegasco, seeing as how I was a girl. Nor did he insinuate, as many others did, that somewhere a man's family was suffering because I had the poor lad's job.

One fellow hadn't bothered to insinuate—he was blunt. Shortly after I was inducted into the union, a Gasco-ite I had not met before, walked up to me while I was loading filters into my truck. "I have a family to support," he said, without introduction.

My backside was sticking out the van door, so I turned, in order to see him and to be certain he was addressing me. He was standard Minnegasco issue—blue shirt and pants, average height, and thinning ash-blond hair. "That's nice," I said.

"I've been working here for ten years," he said slowly. He pulled cigarette smoke through his teeth, making a whistling sound, and peered at me with accusing eyes. "I shoulda had your job. I wanted it."

The posting I had signed in order to get into Buildings and Grounds was a standard one. Union rules required that such postings be distributed companywide. The opportunity to sign it was there for all employees. Wherever he had made his mistake and missed his opportunity was his problem, not mine.

"I was sick when the posting was up. By the time I was back on the job, it was too late. I never got a chance to sign it. I shouldn't hafta suffer just because I was off on sick leave."

"But I should?" I asked.

"You ain't suffering, s'far's I see. You're making more money than me. And Tiny tells me you don't know nothin' 'bout your job, anyhow."

"Thank Tiny for the compliment."

"He wasn't complimenting you!"

"If he said, 'She don't know nothing,' he was." I decided not to explain double negatives. "Besides, what do you know about me? I've never met you. I have a family to support, too," I lied. "Is your family more important than mine? I bet you don't believe in welfare, do you?"

"You're right about that. Goddamngovernmentgiveaways is what's wrong with this country."

"So what should the people who are getting the giveaways do?"

"Kee-rist! They oughta be working! Getting their own goddamn jobs! Why should I hafta support them losers?"

I waited a moment. I wanted him to hear what he had just said. No light bulbs seemed to be coming on, though, so I pushed ahead. "Well, then," I said, smirking, "you need to congratulate me."

"Congratulate you?"

"Yes," I began, wondering why I was wasting my time. I tried a different angle.

"What group of people make up most of the welfare recipients?" I asked.

He was eager to share his knowledge on this subject, as I knew he would be. "Af-fro A-mer-i-kans," he said proudly, drawing out the syllables.

"Wrong, but let's pretend your answer is correct. Shouldn't you be happy that I have a job?" I asked, smiling. "Forgive me, but I don't know your name."

"Bert."

"It's like this, Bert. You can't have it both ways," I said, slamming the van door and walking around to the driver's side. I leaped behind the steering wheel, plugged the key into the ignition, and revved up the engine. "You either accept the welfare system, or you shut up and let me work," I shouted, screeching out of the yard and leaving him in a cloud of blue exhaust fumes.

During a coffee break in the shop one afternoon, Frank was in the middle of a detailed description of a medical procedure involving enemas when Sidney Wimple walked in, much to my relief.

"*There* you are, Peggie!" Sid said, ignoring Frank. Frank obviously didn't mind being ignored. He was up and on his way out the door. "I've been looking for you."

"Hi, Sidney," I said.

"You know where I've been all morning?"

Dumb guessing games, but he was the boss. I had to play. "At a meeting?" I asked. I guessed it was as good a place as any to find a boss.

"Yes, but what *kind* of meeting?" he said, taking a chair across from me.

A moment ago I was listening to Frank talking about enemas, and now I was trapped with Sidney Wimple, playing twenty questions.

"I don't know," I whined, trying unsuccessfully to stop the movement in his paisley tie.

"Sensitivity training!"

Please, not that. "That's nice," I said, standing. "I have to get back to work. I'm sweeping the shop for Sawdust."

"Sit down. That can wait. It was never clean before you gals—er, women—arrived. Gosh, this is so exciting!"

I sat down again, pulled a cigarette from my pack, and lit up. He twitched disapprovingly, but I needed to smoke. He said, "I now know, for instance, why Afro-Americans call themselves *niggers* but get mad when we do. Oh, first, I should ask you: do you prefer *Afro-American* or *black*?"

I hoped Minnegasco wasn't spending too much money on this educational endeavor, considering the results. "May I answer with a question of my own?" I asked.

"Certainly," he said with excitement, sensing a dialogue. It looked to me as though we might be dialoguing for a long time. My stomach felt queasy. I took a deep breath.

"What is your ethnic background?"

"Good question," he said, pushing his glasses up on his nose with a spatulate finger. "I'm a little bit Irish and English, but mostly I'm German, Norwegian, and Swedish."

"So what do I call you? Scandinavian, with a touch of the Irish and a bit of the blue blood? Or do you prefer Western European? Or shall I call you a Caucasian guy?"

"I'm white," he replied without hesitation.

"Good," I said with equal speed. "Call me Peggie. I'm glad we've straightened that out. Guess I'll go back to sweeping."

"No, no! I want you to hear what I've learned! I learned that when you guys call each other *nigger*, you don't really mean it. You're just kidding around and taking ownership of the word so white people don't have the power to make you feel bad when we say it. Isn't that interesting?"

"Oh?"

"Yes, and women can feel the same kind of discrimination in the workplace as blacks do."

"Really?"

"Sure. By golly, it's my job as the boss to see to it that the lines of communication are open. Because so often, problems arise from a simple breakdown in communication. I never thought of that before I took this course. Anyhow, you people speak what's called *Black English*, and we speak regular English, so the lines of communication get broken down because we can't understand what we're saying to each other."

I felt dizzy.

"But wait a minute," he said. "You don't speak with an accent, do you?"

I rolled my eyes in exasperation. "Are you saying I don't speak at all?"

"No, no, no," he said, getting more excited. "I mean, you speak the same way I do."

*I don't think so,* I thought.

"You don't speak Black English."

I sighed. "I'm black. I speak. Therefore, I speak Black English."

"No, you're missing my point. You don't speak with an accent."

"That's impossible."

"No, really. You don't have an accent."

"Sidney, I beg to differ. Every time I say something, I say it with an accent. It may be a Minnesota accent, or a Southern accent, or a Bronx accent. But unless I'm communicating in sign language, I can't speak without some kind of accent." For the first time in my life, I wished I were sweeping a floor.

Sidney tilted his head back and squeezed his face together in a way that made his glasses walk up his nose and fall into place. I resisted the urge to blow smoke in his face and waited for him to tell me what else he had learned. Where was Sonny?

"You know what else I learned? Women often feel as if their intentions are misunderstood. Like when you're wearing a short skirt, it doesn't necessarily mean that it's a come-on."

And so it went. Four hours of sensitivity training. Sidney had learned a lot. He needed to communicate. Finally, he said, "There are three more sessions. I'd love for you to join me. I have an extra ticket, because Lenny said he was too busy to make it. Why don't I clear it with him so you can come with me? I'm sure it would be okay. I mean, you're only sweeping here anyway. It's not like you're doing anything important."

I slumped. The shop went unswept, and I went home with a headache. Luckily for me, Lenny was a man of reason. He said he couldn't spare me.

# 16

## *Changing of the Guard*

EVERYBODY AGREED that Minnegasco was changing. But then, things were changing everywhere. All you had to do was to look in the daily paper to know that.

> *The State University System has agreed to pay a to-tal of $63,000 to 69 women faculty members who claimed they had been underpaid over the past four years, it was announced.*
>
> MINNEAPOLIS TRIBUNE, April 16, 1976

* * *

*The Justice Department Thursday filed its first suits aimed at forcing lending institutions to abandon practices that allegedly discriminate against women in the lending of home mortgage money.*

MINNEAPOLIS TRIBUNE, April 19, 1976

\* \* \*

*Jami Buckner, 18, Westminster, Colo., almost became the first female to attend college on a football scholarship.*

MINNEAPOLIS TRIBUNE, April 29, 1976

At Minnegasco, Rockhead retired. To commemorate the event, Lenny bought a round of coffee for everyone. We took ten minutes to shake Rockhead's hand and wish him well. It was the last time anyone mentioned his name, except for a few years later when his daughter worked a short stint as a summer intern. I felt sorry for her, and not because she looked like her dad, with hair. I felt sorry for her because she had to spend so much time making excuses for him. She tried to justify Rockhead's behavior by explaining that he had dropped out of high school. It sounded to me like a good reason for putting tax dollars into education.

With Rockhead's departure, and a general changing of the guard all over the company, the hostility toward women declined. Buildings and Grounds was no exception. The daytime B&G workforce included two electricians, one carpenter foreman, two pipefitter foremen, eight janitors, two truck drivers, and Rockhead, until he retired. All of them were white men in their late forties or older.

But below them were a host of new helpers and apprentices, all training to be pipefitters. Urbin, Randy, and Marty Hujda, who, like Randy, had joined B&G from an office position, were also white men but were in their mid- to late twenties. And then, for a touch of color and diversity, there were Sonny and me.

Actually, these new white guys brought a different sort of thinking with them. For the most part, their attitudes were more liberated, and they accepted the idea of a diverse workforce more easily. They had wives who worked outside the home, by choice. Randy's wife, Jackie, ran a successful business of her own. Marty's wife, Robin, worked in Minnegasco's downtown office. Judy Mayer kept the books for a small business. The younger generation of B&G'ers saw nothing unusual about this. Their identities weren't threatened by female workers. There was no gender competition when I worked with them, a situation that seemed impossible to duplicate when I was working with some of the older members of the department.

Some of these older men treated me more like a daughter than like a colleague. Sawdust and Bliss, for instance, were courteous and polite, but they didn't take me seriously as a pipefitter. Sawdust never trusted me to be able to take an accurate measurement, or to cut a board straight, or to sand a tabletop. When I worked with Sawdust, I cleaned the shop.

For these older men, and for some of the younger ones, women weren't meant to hoist steel, or crank on a twenty-four-inch pipe wrench, or operate a table saw. But they

would retire long before I would. I could tolerate their idio-
syncrasies until they were gone. I felt no need to object
when they held doors open for me or helped me carry a
heavy load, even though they were positive that I couldn't
have gotten the work done without their assistance. I was
even willing to listen to their suggestions on better ways to
approach a job—many were excellent—as long as the suggestions were delivered respectfully, which they usually
were. I reasoned that as long as I wasn't taking any of these
folks home with me at night, I didn't have to care what they
thought.

Elmo and Box, of course, were different. They continued
to treat me kindly. But it was also clear that they loved to
teach. Nothing made them happier than to be asked le-
gions of questions about a job, especially if the questions
showed that the pupil was learning something. Elmo, in
particular, seemed to understand that he wasn't going to
be at Gasco forever, and he seemed anxious to make sure
that his knowledge was passed on. It really didn't seem to
matter to him whether he passed it on to a man or to a
woman.

In spite of the unpleasant things that had happened, I
liked my work. As I expected would eventually happen, I
was sent to work with JE. But those days were uneventful.
Little was said, and he kept his distance from me. Though
I still preferred to work with Sonny, I didn't need her support in the same way that I had when we'd started. My confidence grew, and I relaxed. Sometimes, in fact, I really let
myself go.

Urbin and I drove out of Minneapolis to several far-northern meter stations once to shovel snow off the sidewalks. Lenny had given us about six work orders, each for a different meter station. We loaded a pickup truck with a snowblower, a couple of shovels, and bags of salt and sand mix. I filled my Thermos with coffee, grabbed my lunch bag, and jumped into the passenger seat.

As we made our way out of the city, it started to snow. The snow settled delicately on tree branches, dressing them with a fresh blanket of white. We both enjoyed the quiet, away from the city. Urbin began to hum a tune, and then, as if he were at home alone in his shower, he began to sing.

*In a lit-tle ca-fe just the o-ther side of the bor-der . . .*

I was happy he had chosen a song I knew, and one that had a good female part. I waited, eagerly anticipating my solo.

*She-was-a-sit-ting there a-giv-ing me looks that made*
*    my mouth wa-ter . . .*
*So I star-ted wal-king her way . . .*
*She be-longed to Bad Man Jose . . .*
*And I knew-ew yes I knew-ew I should run,*
*But then I heard her say-yay-yay . . . .*

I blew myself up and belted in my best soprano voice:

*Come a lit-tle bit clo-ser, you're my kin-da guy-eye*
*So big and so stro-ong,*
*Come a lit-tle bit clo-ser, I'm all a-lone*
*And the night is so long . . . .*

The pickup swerved off the road. Urbin pulled wildly at the steering wheel and got it under control. He brought the truck to a pulsating stop. "What the hell was *that*?" he yelled, looking at me with bugged-out eyes and a barely controlled grin.

Then he started laughing. And he laughed and laughed, holding his stomach and wiping tears from his eyes. Between tears and choppy gasps for breath he croaked, "I ain't *never* heard anything like that before. Holy Mother of God, you better register that thing! It's *lethal*!"

"I can sing," I said defensively as he started the truck and steered it back onto the road. My comment set off a new round of hysterics. "Hey," I said, "it wasn't that bad!"

This wasn't exactly true, though. As much as I loved to sing, I was used to similar reactions, though usually not quite so extreme.

Urbin and I started to sing together all the time. Much later, Steve the Sewerman joined us and we formed a sort of group. Between them, Urbin and Steve knew the words to every show tune ever written, and they both favored Robert Goulet-type songs. I knew the tunes, but I wasn't much good with the words. So I made them up. They soon got used to my methods and gave up trying to correct me. We were entertainers and audience rolled into one. We weren't even average, but we had loads of fun.

Marty didn't sing. But much later, in the 1980s, he liked to tell stories. Specifically, he liked to recount the plots of his two favorite prime-time soap operas, *Falcon Crest* and *Flamingo Road*.

"Aha, let's see," he'd begin before starting his van. Marty was also a weekend race car driver, but he didn't race in a

Gasco van. "Where did we leave off?" It was a rhetorical question. Marty knew his soaps. He would retell each episode in the greatest detail. I never watched the shows myself, but I couldn't wait for the day after both of them aired, knowing that Marty was sure to do a blow-by-blow account.

"Oh yes, oh yes. Marla . . . now you remember, she's the one with the, ah . . . with the, ah . . ." Marty outlined an invisible arc over his chest and grinned slyly.

"Breasts. They're called breasts," I said.

"Knockers," he said, not skipping a beat. "She was in love with Tom, but he's in love with Marla's twin sister, Karla, but Marla doesn't care anymore because she fell in love with Tom's father, who she met in the hospital when she was taking care of him after a small case of pneumonia." Marty looked at me seriously and added, "You do remember, don't you, that Marla is a nurse?" Or some such. I never remembered the details, I just loved the way he told the stories.

I tried, but I couldn't get Randy to sing. He and Jackie were busy building a new home, from the ground up. Randy and I talked about social issues. Women's issues. Children. Minnegasco politics. We never solved anything, but we sure enjoyed trying.

But singing, storytelling, and politics while I worked weren't the only things that had changed for me. Two years after I started working for Minnegasco, I took and passed the pipefitter's licensing test.

Sidney Wimple had a story of his own to tell on the day

the gas company was informed that they employed the first female pipefitter in the state of Minnesota.

Lenny called me into the office to give me the good news. "Sid and I didn't want to upset you by telling you what the guy at the testing board said when we sent in your application," he said, smiling into his coffee mug.

"What'd he say?" I asked.

Just then, Sidney poked his head over the partition that separated him from Lenny, hanging his arms over the parts not occupied by his philodendron. "I'll tell you what he said," Sidney said enthusiastically. "First, Lenny sent in your application. It said your name was *Margaret*, of course. The dope down at the testing board sent it back, didn't he, Lenny?" Lenny nodded.

"He told Lenny we must have made a mistake. He told Lenny we must have meant *Michael*. Lenny straightened him out. After which, he told Lenny that the pipefitter's exam had never been given to a woman in the whole history of the test!"

Sidney waited, but nobody said anything. He shrugged and went on, "So you know what Lenny said?"

"No," I said, wishing he'd let Lenny tell his own story. "What did Lenny say?"

"Lenny here said, 'It's about time, don't you think?'"

# 17

## *The Silver Fox*

IT WAS OFFICIAL. I was a pipefitter. Not a trainee but a real pipefitter. What did this mean?

Well, for one thing, my wallet would now have four identification cards in it, not just three. Driver's license. Social Security card. Library card. Pipefitter's license. It meant that I'd be a pipefitter for as long as I paid my yearly dues. And last, but perhaps most important, it meant a raise in pay.

I felt a sense of pride in having accomplished something no other woman in the state had done. I also felt silly about being proud. It was a pipefitter's license, after all, not a medical degree. Even so, I grinned a lot in those first few days.

When I told Mom about it, she momentarily halted her campaign to get me out of Minnegasco and beamed with maternal pride. She phoned her friends to inform them that her daughter was the only female pipefitter in the state.

"You know, Mom," I said, "there are probably lots of women out there doing pipefitter work, with a lot more knowledge and skill than I've got."

"Yes, dear," she said, "but you're the only one with a diploma."

Not everybody shared her excitement about the event. Tiny congratulated me by hocking another gob of phlegm at my feet. I was furious. A couple of the welded-together boys had to haul him away from me as he hollered something about faggot lady libbers screwing everything up. I thought about reporting his behavior to Lenny, but I didn't.

With two years in at the gas company, and with a pipefitter's license in my pocket, I still had no faith in the ability of the company's male hierarchy to understand the extent of my outrage, and to do something more than scold men like Tiny for their actions. Lenny, of course, would understand, but anything that happened to Tiny would have to come from two or three rungs farther up the corporate ladder, where I didn't know anybody. Nothing short of his being suspended without pay, or fired, would have satisfied my sense of fairness.

It was also true that a number of men, including Tiny, had tried and failed many times to pass the pipefitter's license test. My license gave me a much better job than Tiny's, even though he had worked for the gas company nearly thirty years. Since we worked in different departments, it was unlikely that we would ever compete for the same job. But it obviously bothered him to know that if we did, I'd get it and he wouldn't. I could live with that.

My new license also brought new responsibilities.

Lenny found an old truck and declared it officially mine. He had it fitted with a top, and I loaded it with furnace filters. Then, in addition to my other duties, he issued me a standing order to replace all the filters in every air-handling unit in the company when they needed it. I was immediately dubbed the Filter Queen.

Changing filters wasn't hard, and in some odd way that I think had to do with the freedom the job gave me, I enjoyed it. Sometimes, changing filters required a touch of ingenuity. Occasionally, I even had to get inside an air-handling unit in order to change the filter. And since some of the cooling and heating units were custom made, I often had to fabricate filters that couldn't be bought off the rack.

The air handler in the Linden garage was one of the biggest in the system. Lenny and I designed a frame to hold a large batt of synthetic filter material and used twisters— like those used on bread bags—to hold the material to the frame. Once the material was secured, I had to wrestle the makeshift filter up a ladder and into the huge air-handler, which hung from the ceiling of the garage. In order to set the filter properly, I had to crawl all the way into the unit. From ground level, only my feet were visible.

My new responsibilities also included testing and treating the water in the air-conditioning system at the Linden Building.

"How does one test and treat water?" Mom asked, sitting across from me in her kitchenette. We were drinking coffee, and I knew she didn't really want to know about water testing. I suspected a ploy, and that soon we'd be talking about journalism. Her indifference annoyed me, because I *liked* testing the water. I decided to give her the long explanation.

"I use a test tube to get a small sample of water," I said, taking a sip of coffee from a china cup. I flashed a smile her way and continued. "I get the sample from the bleed valve. You see, every system has a bleed valve, in order to release water pressure when necessary, or to drain samples of water . . ."

"I know that," Mom interrupted. "I have done extensive research on boilers and air conditioners and heating options. I know all about solar heating, too."

"Liar," I said, grinning. "Anyway, as I was saying before I got interrupted, I've got a little blue chemistry set. You know—the kind that you and Dad used to give Randy every Christmas."

Mom winced. One Christmas, when my younger brother Randy was about seven, my parents gave him a chemistry set. Prominently displayed on the packaging were the words FOR CHILDREN AGED TEN OR OLDER. My parents were convinced that Randy was advanced for his age.

Randy nearly burned the house down. Undaunted, my parents bought him another set. This time he set out to see how long it would take—applying different concoctions of his own making to books he selected from Mom's library—to get paper to burn. Not long, he discovered.

The following Christmas, Mom sewed Randy a bathrobe.

Mom didn't like being reminded of chemistry sets, and I knew it.

I continued to explain. "I set the test tube in a tray. Then I put the water sample through a series of tests, using different chemicals." I waited for her to ask what chemicals I used, but the question didn't come. "Anyhow, from the test results, I determine what, if any, chemicals I should add to the system."

"Mmm," Mom said. "What you're saying is that you are no longer a nipplefitter. You are a chemist. That sounds much nicer."

Armed with my pipefitter's license, my water-test kit, and my new nickname, I went to work with a pride I never expected to feel from working at Minnegasco. I discovered that I liked the gratification of having my own projects, started, solved, and completed on the same day. It was very different from procrastinating a week before writing a term paper, or having to work under Rockhead's direction.

I liked working with my hands. I liked testing the water, and having my own truck, and being independent. But could I be satisfied with a career at Minnegasco? Could I hide a career at Minnegasco from my mother?

"Whaddya mean, drop out of school?" Sonny shouted in disbelief. "Are you crazy? What will your mom say? It'd kill her!"

"I haven't discussed it with her," I said.

Sonny was taping a FEMALE AT WORK sign on the door of the basement men's room at the Linden Building. Once again, the Bradley fountain had stopped working. It failed with such frequency that I began to suspect sabotage. Sonny turned to face me and grinned sarcastically.

"Trying to work up the courage to tell her you dropped out?" she asked.

By then Sonny and Mom had met—and liked each other.

"Why don't you talk to her first? You two buddies can knock the idea around for a while, and then you can make my decision for me," I said, banging on the men's room door. "Hell-o! Anyone in there?" One grunt. "Sorry! We'll wait!"

I looked at Sonny. "I'm making good money here. I'd never make this kind of money from studying German history or communications or statistics. Especially statistics. I passed that class, but the only thing I can tell you about statistics is that they don't mean much."

"Yeah," Sonny smirked. "Unless you happen to be a politician."

The last men's room occupant emerged, red-faced. He scooted past us without a word and flew up the steps. Sonny and I went in to assess the damage. I pressed the foot pedal on the Bradley fountain. It didn't spring back, nor did it release water the way it should have. Instead, the pedal lay flat on the floor like a dead soldier.

I scratched my head. "Spring's busted, I think. Let's get the panel off and find out what we have here." I pulled a fancy scroogie from the tool belt that hung over my shoulder. We unscrewed the panel and spotted the trouble.

"Why aren't *you* in school?" I asked, taking apart the spring-loaded bolt and cotter pin. It was clear that we would have to go to a plumbing-supply company to get replacement parts.

"Soon as I pay a couple bills I plan to go back to school," she said. "I've already got a year in. Think I'd like to get a degree in social work."

"Why social work?" I asked. "They're all white women from the suburbs. All they do is butt into other people's business and preach at them, especially if they're poor. I can't see you doing that."

"I like doing things that people can't see me doing," she said seriously. "Besides, maybe there's a better way to do social work."

Well, why not? She was street-smart, and book-smart, and definitely not from the suburbs.

"I started out wanting to be a political speechwriter," I said, hanging an OUT OF ORDER sign on the Bradley.

"You really think we need that sign?" Sonny asked. "Most of the Bradley is lying on the floor."

"We need the sign," I said. "Let's go shopping. I'll drive."

"I wanted to ghostwrite speeches," I said in the truck

on the way to Goodin Plumbing Supply. "I worked for Humphrey in '68, and McGovern in '72. I went with my mother to all sorts of Democratic rallies and conventions and dinners. Mostly I made phone calls and knocked on doors and listened to speeches. Lots of speeches. I learned that the political life is definitely not for me. So I changed from journalism to communications, with a minor in history."

"What do you plan to do with a communications degree?" Sonny asked.

It was a question I had asked myself on many occasions, but I still had no answer. "I don't know. Fit pipes, maybe."

Sonny and I made our purchase and drove back to Linden. We replaced the broken foot pedal parts and put the Bradley fountain back together. We were sitting in the lunchroom on our lunch break when Urbin walked over to us. He was working a cuticle stick under his fingernails. "Hey, Filter Queen, the guys upstairs are looking for you," he said.

"What do they want?"

"Dunno."

"Who wants me?"

"Carlson."

Carlson? What could Dick Carlson want with me? I stared at Sonny. She shrugged, pulled a book from a brown paper bag, and began to read, losing interest in me. I gathered my lunch bag and Thermos and took the elevator to the second floor.

I went around the corner and into the upstairs lunchroom. This was unofficially the office workers' lunchroom. I could hear the sound of male voices.

Dick Carlson was easy to spot. He was tall and lean, in his mid-fifties. A polo player swung a mallet on the breast of his neat white cardigan. I figured he wore a whole team of them in places I couldn't see. A pair of Coke-bottle-bottom glasses was perched on his aristocratic nose. I watched him as he blew a slowly rising smoke ring and ran a hand through his wavy silver hair. They called him the Silver Fox because of it. He was shuffling a deck of cards.

The Fox had a reputation for being one of the best card-players at the gas company. This was a matter of no small prestige in a place where card games took up just about everybody's breaks, and often longer. The Fox never took extended breaks, though. When break time was officially over, he went back to preparing maps and routings for the leak-detection crews.

The Fox and two other men were about to begin a game.

"There you are," he said when he saw me standing in the doorway. "Urbin said you were here. We need a fourth for cribbage. Would you like to play?"

"Cribbage? Me?" Why would he want me to play with them? We hardly knew each other. We'd barely spoken. My Gasco cardplaying was limited to a supporting role in a game of five hundred in the basement lunchroom with Mickey. I'd watched these people play. They played incredibly fast. No endless streams of delirious babbling, as in the games downstairs.

"I've never played before," I said. "Everything I know

about cribbage I learned watching you guys. Are you sure you want me?"

"I watched you and Mickey play five hundred the other day."

I remembered. Mickey and I had played two games against a couple of fast-talking meter repairmen. The repair guys soon learned that loud razzing wouldn't save them from Mickey, and they left in a silent hurry after losing both games by a wide margin. I hadn't done much except follow Mickey's lead, but I walked away with fifty cents.

"Looked like you have good card sense," the Fox continued. "Looked like you're a fast study." He turned his head to one side. "Anyway, I need a partner. Why don't you sit down, and we'll see what we can do?"

There were two ways to participate in the sport of cribbage at the gas company, and only one of them was playing. The other, which happened only when the best players were playing, was kibitzing. When the Fox played cards, a crowd usually gathered. I'd ooed and aahed plenty of times at the Silver Fox's card table. But to sit down at that table was a big jump.

The Fox put a cup of coffee in my hand and gestured for me to sit across from him. To avoid making a scene, I sat down. "She's in," I heard someone say. Instantly, a crowd formed. Where all these spectators had been hiding, I had no idea.

Our opponents were not exactly slouches. The first was a wiry little man with buck teeth named Squinty, a senior clerk in the Service Department. Squinty lived in a cloud of smoke. He used one cigarette to light the next and never seemed to take them out of his mouth, even to flick ashes into an ashtray. Squinty narrowed his eyes and blew out a white puff of smoke. "Welcome," he said, coughing.

The fourth player, Fred, was a Street Department dispatcher. Fred was as large as Squinty was small. Fred smoked, too, but he interrupted his smoking to eat doughnuts, or candy bars, or popcorn, or anything else he could find. He wiped a spot of sugar from his lips. "Good luck, honey," he said in a rich voice. He winked, as if to say I'd need it. *Well, we'll just see,* I thought, with fading confidence. I was completely out of my league, and on the wrong floor.

The laborers played cards in the basement. We were raucous and relaxed. We played on church-basement trestle tables, the kind with peeling Formica tops and wads of gum stuck underneath. Up here, they played at clean little malt-shop tables. They played silently, like accountants. I wondered again why Dick Carlson had called for me.

The Fox and Squinty cut for deal, and Squinty won. He dealt a round of cards so fast that all I saw was a blue blur at the end of his arm.

Squinty coughed and sat back to scrutinize the cards he had given himself. No one spoke. My heart pounded so loudly I was sure they could hear it, but the three men were intent on their own hands. The Fox quickly threw a card into Squinty's crib. So did Fred. Nobody paid any attention to me.

I fanned the five cards in my hand. Two sevens. Two

eights. A three. I had a no-brainer. I put the three in the pile next to Squinty.

Now, what was next? Fifteen and thirty-one were the numbers I needed to remember.

Squinty put a card into his crib and flipped up the top card of the already-cut deck. Four of hearts. *Oh no*, I thought. I had given Squinty a three, and it was too late to retrieve it. I hoped that Fred and Squinty hadn't put fives in the pile. Or deuces.

"Two," my partner said, putting the deuce of spades down on the table.

"Eight," said Fred, flipping down the six of diamonds.

"Fifteen," I said, laying down one of my sevens. A murmur went up behind me. The Fox pegged two holes. We were off and running.

Squinty smiled. "Twenty-three for three," he said, snapping down the eight of clubs. With my two, three eights were accounted for. Where was the fourth?

The corners of Dick's mouth went up ever so slightly. "Thirty-one for four," he said quietly, laying down the last eight. He moved our peg four holes. We'd pegged six to their three.

"Ooo. Aah." The spectators sounded like the male equivalent of women at a baby shower, right after the mom-to-be opens her first pair of blue booties.

"Thought you said she didn't play, Dick," Fred said, squinting like Squinty.

"I said she *didn't* play," the Fox said, smiling at me. "I didn't say she *couldn't* play."

We played three games and lost one. I never held a hand worth less than seven holes that day and never misplayed. Better still, the Fox and I seemed to be instinctively playing into each other. What he didn't have, I had, and vice versa. My confidence soared, and after that first set of games, I became a regular at the Fox's table whenever I was at the Linden Building and his usual partner was missing.

"I knew you were a fast study," the Fox said, approvingly. "By the way, have you met my son yet?"

A son? Working here? A young Fox? Well, if he was like his father—an attractive prospect, I had to admit—he was probably married. Eventually we would meet and we would be friends, as I was with his dad. Boy-girl stuff would have been too complicated anyway: not just a work romance but an interracial one as well. No way. But here I was, conjuring up a doomed relationship with a man I hadn't met.

"I don't think so," I said. "Should I have?"

"He works in your department."

I didn't know anyone named Carlson. I sure didn't know anyone, except for Elmo when he was cleaned up, who looked anything like the Silver Fox. I ran a mental inventory of every B&G'er I could think of. Nope. I couldn't put a son with this father. "I can't place him," I said disappointedly.

"I think you'd like him," the Fox said.

"Really? Why?" I asked with renewed interest and perhaps too much enthusiasm.

"You read a lot, I've noticed," he said in his quiet voice, as if it was supposed to be a secret. "Dick reads a lot, too. He's the night janitor here. Gives him lots of time to read."

Well, Mom would approve of his pastime, at least. But we couldn't be talking relationships here.

"History, mostly. He majored in it at the University of Minnesota. Damned if I can understand sometimes why he's still working here."

That settled it. I'd have to work overtime at Linden some evening.

# 18

## One of Us Is Pregnant

"UMM, BEFORE YOU GO back to the shop, I have a short announcement to make," Lenny said after completing the question-and-answer segment of the safety meeting.

"Kee-*rist*, you mean this meeting ain't over yet?" Bliss whined from the back of the room.

"This will only take a minute," Lenny said, turning red. "Randy, will you please wake up Box?" Lenny pecked nervously at his Vikings mug and waited. Randy kicked Box's chair. Box jerked back to life.

Lenny took a deep breath and sighed. "One of us is pregnant," he said.

I knew he was going to have to tell the others soon, or wait for them to figure it out themselves. Meanwhile, there were things an expectant mother wasn't supposed to do, like work around toxic fumes, or climb too high up a ladder, or lift a loaded toolbox.

I smiled, revealing nothing, as our colleagues scrutinized Sonny's and my midsections and silently speculated. One of us was engaged in premarital sex, or the other was no longer separated from her husband. Or maybe something even more unthinkable was going on. Sonny and I were, respectively, twenty-two and twenty-four years old, which made us both prime candidates. She sat next to me, also smiling. We both knew that the B&G oddsmakers would name her as the more likely new mother. Pregnancy would explain why she had suddenly started wearing baggy bib overalls and oversized shirts.

"Well, it wasn't too easy, but I finally convinced those jokers down at Personnel that we could make a spot for someone on limited duty. It's not like this is a new issue, given all the back injuries we get. So we've added a full-time position for a lunchroom attendant at the Linden Building. You know, somebody to keep the place clean and to be on hand to make fresh coffee. Lord knows we get enough complaints about that swill we serve over there. Anyhow," Lenny continued, stopping a minute to empty his mug, "the requirements for the new position will be the same as they are for the downtown lunchroom attendant. Then, if the occasion should arise again anytime soon—I mean another pregnancy," he nodded in my direction, and got even redder, "we'll have a full-time job for the person." He stared into his empty mug and added, "Or for any limited-duty guy, too."

"Any of you guys planning on getting knocked up?" Urbin asked. Everyone laughed, even Lenny.

"No need to make provisions for me," I muttered.

I thought there would be a great deal of complaining among the men about how pregnant-out-of-wedlock girls shouldn't get to do ladies' work and still make a man's wage. But I was wrong. Not a voice was raised in protest. Plenty of protests came later, from outside our department, but I didn't concern myself with them.

Box stuck his hand up as if he were in grade school and under strict orders not to speak unless called upon.

"Yes, Robert?" Lenny said.

"So when's the new little fitter due?" he asked.

"Five and a half months," Sonny said, ending any debate over which one of us was the new mother. Thankfully, nobody asked who the new little fitter's father was. Had they known he was black, the conclusion of the safety meeting wouldn't have been so cordial.

Sonny's romance originated in the company's decision to embark on a complete renovation of all its facilities at the same time that the Linden Building was being put through some major structural changes. When it became clear that Buildings and Grounds didn't have enough staff to handle these jobs alone and still keep the rest of the company's regular maintenance, Lenny hired professional painters to help us.

The day that Lamar Lockhart stuck his nose into Sonny's and my business, we were repainting a support pillar in the Linden lunchroom. We were painting it blue, after one of the contract painters had mistakenly painted it green.

"That's not how to paint rough brick, ladies."

We both turned toward the booming voice. It came from a giant man who stood, hands on hips, smiling a smile that wrapped around his tan face like a car bumper, long and thick. He might have been twenty-six, but no older. Baggy painter's coveralls couldn't hide the fact that he was in good shape. Black eyes, deep-cut dimples, and a big bushy beard made this painter look more like a lumberjack.

As usual, Sonny beat me to the punch. "I suppose you know how to paint this thing the right way?" she asked, with a flirty little grin I'd never seen.

"I'll just use your brush, darlin'," he said, easily slipping Sonny's paintbrush from her hand. I had never seen her relent like that before. It was disgusting. Within a couple of months it became clear that she had kept on relenting to Lamar—or, just as likely, he'd been relenting to her. And now they were going to be parents.

It was beginning to seem as if everybody was paired up, like shoes and socks. I had been wearing my wedding band to ward off unwanted advances. But everyone I'd met at Minnegasco was either happily or unhappily involved, so I didn't need it.

The few times I had been tentatively asked whether I was married or single, I had answered yes with a toothy smile. The curious were left scratching their heads.

Though I continued to tell myself that I was not interested in becoming involved in a Minnegasco relationship, I wondered how my future would look without a relationship of any kind, Minnegasco or otherwise. I knew I wanted three things: a college degree, a real husband, and children. None of them looked likely to happen if I remained at Minnegasco. So for the time being, I stuffed my hopes and desires, put on a smiling face, and kept plodding ahead.

During those days at Minnegasco, I spent most of my time at the Linden Building: checking the quality of the water in the air-handling units, changing filters, repairing Bradley fountains, tearing down office partitions and putting them up again, and moving office furniture around.

The moving chores were the most annoying of the lot. It seemed as though every time we'd get some guy settled into one spot, he'd be promoted, or he'd retire, or he'd want to move away from the air vents, or next to them, or he'd die and his replacement would hate the dead guy's office furniture.

Worst of all were the guys who complained because their offices were smaller than the office of some other guy who had less seniority than they did. Work order after work order would instruct me to move Joe Doakes's office partition three feet north and give him a window. The obvious answer to these problems, it seemed to me, would have been to tell the whiners to stop whining and wait six months for the inevitable next renovation. But Minnegasco's corporate culture valued seniority above everything, even among the managers.

So I was kept busy, spinning in place, keeping management and the office dwellers happy. In the middle of all this madness, some guy (who probably had a B.S. degree in how to build worker morale by Inventing Stupid Games) started a contest to come up with a slogan to commemorate the renovation. The winner was MOVING, GROWING, CHANGING, with emphasis on the M, the G, and the C. As in M-inneapolis G-as C-ompany.

The corporate types liked the new slogan so much, they ordered MOVING, GROWING, CHANGING T-shirts and coffee mugs and ashtrays and notepads and pens and a bunch of other tacky knickknacks, and distributed them companywide. This was supposed to do something for employee morale. Judging from the comments of the frustrated office workers, it did indeed affect morale but not how the company had envisioned.

In order to save wear and tear on my knees, I used the only passenger elevator in the Linden Building as often as I could, though it was famous for breaking down frequently. Nobody dared to use it on Fridays, for fear of being stuck in it all weekend. On the other hand, being stuck on company time wasn't too bad, as long as you had a good book.

I was in the temperamental elevator with Dick Carlson one day when it lurched upward and then dropped about a foot before slowly fizzling to a stop. The Silver Fox and I were both familiar with the signs. It was a Wednesday afternoon. There was plenty of time to wait for someone to repair the elevator.

The Fox grabbed the emergency telephone and followed the instructions posted in officious-looking black handwritten letters next to the red emergency phone box. *Take deep breaths. Remain calm. Dial 333. State clearly which building you are in. A serviceman will arrive soon.*

"We're in the Linden Building elevator!" he shouted into the receiver. "At Minnegasco! 700 Linden Avenue West! No, it's in Minneapolis!" He hung up the phone. "Knuckleheads. They get calls from here five times a week, and we gotta tell them where we are?

"Why don't you sit down?" he said in a friendlier tone. "These guys don't know the meaning of *soon*." He jabbed the word on the sign with a long bony finger.

From the floor I watched him stare into his empty coffee mug. "Well, we're not in the desert, after all. Guess we won't need provisions." I shook my head. "And the company's good, too."

*Indeed it is,* I thought.

"My son has a notion to become a serviceman now," he said, taking up the conversation where we'd left off after our last cribbage game. "Hard to figure why. He's done just about every entry-level job in the company. Night janitor, day janitor, night security. My wife, Lucille, says he oughtta go back to school and get a graduate degree and be a college professor like he used to talk about doing. But she doesn't like to make too big a deal about it because she knows Dick will do what's best for himself. He's held a job ever since he was thirteen. We never had to pay anything to put him through school. He paid to go to De La Salle High School all by himself." He smiled and went right on bragging like the proud parent he was. "We never had to get him out of jail after some war protest, even though he was in a few—protests, I mean, not jails. He's the one kid who's never given us a lick of trouble."

Little Dicky Two Shoes was beginning to sound like a bore. I wished the Fox would tell me about the kids who *had* given Lucille and him a lick of trouble. I was certain they'd be more interesting. But I supposed he felt it was necessary to set up his son for a positive first impression in case I should meet the night janitor.

"How did you come to work here?" he asked.

I had a number of answers ready for this question, most of them defensive and pretty sarcastic. He wasn't going to hear any of them. There was something about him, in his eyes and in his manner. He was honest. I liked that.

"I was in school," I said. "I ran out of money and needed to do something fast. I found out from a telephone installer that the three utilities were going to have to start hiring women. I'm still here because the money is good," I concluded. "What brought you here?"

"The gas company sort of saved us," he said. "I had a real good job at the Twin City Ordnance Plant. I was an office supervisor. Then about twenty years ago, a recession came along. They said the government was going to shut the plant down because of the recession, but most everybody knew it was really because of politics. See, Minnesota was a

Democratic state at that time, and this was during the Eisenhower years, when the Republicans were in power. Anyway, the government gave its contracts to some company in a Republican state. The plant shut down. All of a sudden, I was thirty-seven, with three kids, and out of a job.

"I waited tables for about three months," he said. Then he added sheepishly, "Hell, I was too old and horsy-looking to get good tips. I was lucky to catch on here. This is a great place to work."

"Did you fight in the war?" I didn't want to compare notes with him on the Minnegasco experience, so I changed the subject. I knew I didn't need to specify *which* war. Men who had fought in World War II, I'd learned, simply called it the War.

He sat silently for a long while. Then he said, "Yeah, I did. But I'm glad Dick didn't have to go to Vietnam. I used to get mad at him over his war protesting and his long hair. But I'd never have let him go over there. Never. I'd have sent him to Canada first."

Someone from above pounded on the door. "Anybody down there?" a voice shouted.

I was on my feet in an instant, startled. The Fox smiled and waved a hand, motioning for me to sit. "Yeah, Squinty!" he shouted. "It's me! Dick! Peggie's down here with me, too! I called the knuckleheads. Any sign of them up there yet?"

"Hell, no! You guys got cards?"

"No."

"Sorry ta hear that. See ya later!"

"That," the Fox said, unnecessarily, "was Squinty."

We sat quietly for a while. Squinty's interruption had thrown our conversation off track. I didn't feel uncomfortable being quiet with him. I thought of all the people I could have gotten stuck in the elevator with and was grateful it had been Dick.

Feeling a need to finish the conversation, though, I said, "This may be a great place for you to work, but for me it's kind of a trap. I'm making so much moola, I can't quit."

The Fox laughed. "I think my son's got the same problem," he said.

# 19

## The Hot Item

I WAS IN THE LINDEN BASEMENT, walking toward the enter-at-your-own-risk elevator and juggling a stack of filters for the third-floor air-handling units. Out of the corner of my eye I noticed one of the new guys, sitting at a lunchroom table. Larry Welch was in the Customer Service Department training program.

Customer Service was Minnegasco's elite department. Its skilled servicemen (there were no women) were as highly regarded as meter readers were not. They fixed stoves, furnaces, clothes dryers, air conditioners, and water heaters for Minnegasco customers. The work was highly technical.

I pushed the up button on the elevator and turned to wave at Larry. He waved back and motioned for me to join him. It was almost break time anyway, so I put the pile of filters next to the elevator and sauntered into the lunchroom.

Larry was tall and lean, assertive and intelligent, and he loved controversy. He would argue about any subject, anytime, with inexhaustible passion. His wife, Charlene, worked in Minnegasco's Gas Control Department. She was as tall as he was, with penetrating green eyes, and cover-girl beautiful. When they were together, they turned the heads of passersby. It was somehow liberating to know that this self-possessed black couple were taking a place in the company.

Larry said, "Sit down here. I want you to meet somebody." I sat down, and he waved a long-fingered hand in the direction of a young man clad in the standard blue uniform.

I had all I could do to hide my surprise. The man making his way through the lunchroom to join us was a much younger version of the Silver Fox. He had the same thick, wavy hair, but it was sandy brown, not silver. He had the same blue eyes.

Young Dick Carlson—for this man could be nobody else—wore glasses that were thicker than his father's. They made him look like the student and war protester that his father had described. He sure didn't look like what I'd come to expect from Minnegasco.

In his best game-show host manner, Larry said, "Peggie, this is Dick Carlson." I had learned that Dick was divorced, and Larry had wheedled out of me most of the particulars of my marital status, so I suspected that he was engaged in a bit of matchmaking. I almost laughed out loud at the irony of being corralled to meet someone I had been trying to run into.

"Hello," Dick said. "Dad says you're an excellent card-player." The directness of his manner reminded me of his father.

"He's very kind," I said, somehow relieved to know that his father had talked to him about me. I wouldn't have to pretend that I didn't know anything about him, though I wondered what else his dad might have said to him. I dismissed my concern almost as fast as it had arisen. The Silver Fox was too classy to engage in tabloid gossip or speculation about me. "Your dad is also the best card teacher I've ever met," I said. "He seems like a very patient man."

A nod. "He can be," the son said, crinkling up his eyes. "On the other hand, you ought to see him stuck in traffic. Or worse yet, with a hammer in his hand. You wouldn't believe it was the same guy."

"I thought you worked at night," I said, making no bones about the fact that I had information about him, as well.

"I did, but I got out of B&G. Now I'm in serviceman's school."

Service training was rigorous and was usually viewed as

a career move. It appeared that Dick was going to chuck his liberal arts degree and become a Minnegasco lifer. Mom would never approve.

There followed a long pause, which Larry eventually broke by standing and announcing that he had to leave. "I'll catch you later," he said. *So you two can be alone to-gether* was the obvious implication in his tone. With his love of controversy, I could see Larry being amused at the idea of a white man and a black woman being paired up at Minnegasco.

"Your dad said you have a degree from the U of M," I said to Dick.

"History. Not very practical. I got it after majoring in about six other things. At least it kept me out of Nam. I hear you're thinking about quitting school for a while. How come?"

He surprised me with his knowledge. I wasn't prepared to talk to him about my faltering college experience, and I wondered who had snitched on me. Larry, I guessed, by way of Sonny. "It's a long story," I said. "Are you planning on staying here forever?"

Dick grinned, suddenly looking very much like his father. "Did my mother tell you to ask me that question?"

"I'm sorry," I blurted. "I guess I got caught up in comparing what I thought you'd say with what your father has already told me."

I froze. What had I done? I could not believe the words that sometimes poured from my out-of-control mouth, especially when I was nervous. And I *was* nervous! I could feel his eyes searching mine, and I knew he must think I was a fool. I started to get up.

"Where are you going?" he asked, in a gentle voice.

"Well . . . well I thought, after . . ." The problem, of course, was that I hadn't thought. I dropped back into my chair. "May I start over?" I asked.

"Hello," he laughed, sticking out a hand to shake. "My name is Dick."

"Peggie," I said. "What are you reading these days?"

Dick pulled a paperback copy of *Slaughterhouse Five* by Kurt Vonnegut from his jacket pocket and handed it to me. "I finished it earlier today," he said.

"Is it any good?" I asked, turning it over to read the blurbs on the back cover.

"Keep it," he said. "Then, when you've finished reading it, you can tell me yourself if it's any good."

I hadn't gotten around to Vonnegut yet, but he was on my list. I agreed to the conditions and thanked Dick. We parted, he to class and I to filters.

That night when Mom called, I said nothing about any Carlsons, and I tried not to ask myself why I was afraid to talk about what was only, after all, an innocent conversation.

The trouble with this innocent conversation was that I kept replaying it over and over in my mind. The more I replayed it, the more certain I was that I'd made a dumb impression, and the more distressed I became. The more distressed I became, the more distressed I became about being distressed. Had I already blown it with this interesting man? I didn't go to bed until four in the morning, and even then I didn't sleep.

The first thing that went wrong the next day was that Lenny told me to go with Elmo and Urbin to the Linden Building to help move a bunch of executives into their new offices. Linden was the last place I wanted to be, but I didn't really have a choice. I leaped into the passenger side of my truck and handed Urbin my keys. A minute later I was asleep.

Two seconds later, it seemed, I woke to the sound of the truck's engine being turned off. I opened one eye, self-consciously wiped saliva from the corner of my mouth, and followed Urbin to the second floor to await instructions from Elmo. At least I wasn't likely to encounter the younger Dick Carlson on the second floor.

"You gonna be any help here today?" Urbin asked, with narrow-eyed suspicion.

"Back off," I scowled. "I'm going to the ladies' room," I said, shoving past Urbin and nearly crashing into Elmo as he rounded the corner.

"What's wrong with her?" I heard Elmo ask Urbin.

"Aw, it's probably just her time of the month. They're a crazy species then."

That *really* made me mad. Why do guys always think that if a woman is angry it's because she's menstruating? Are we to believe from this logic that men menstruate, too? God knows they get angry often enough.

I went into the women's rest room, which had a toilet, a new sink, running water, and cream-colored decor, and splashed water on my face. It helped.

I looked in the mirror and asked myself why I was mad. I was mad because I was tired, and because I'd acted like a fool when I'd hoped to make my best impression. The fault was mine alone.

I left the rest room and went into the second-floor lunchroom to get a cup of coffee. Sonny was wiping stains off the counter and putting out new swizzle sticks. "Got a slosh here for ya," she said, handing me a hot Styrofoam cup. "I was going to bring it to you. Saw you going into the rest room. Urbin said you might need a whole pot of the stuff. Is he right? You haven't been drinking again, have you?"

"No, it's not that," I said dejectedly. "He's probably right about the whole pot of coffee, though. Thanks. I've got to go. I've got something that I have to work off. I'll tell you about it at lunch." I moved sullenly toward the door.

"Does it have anything to do with Dick Carlson?" Sonny asked, swinging her dishrag in circles.

I stopped and turned. How could she know? "Where the hell did you get an idea like that?" I demanded.

"Larry told me. Said you two were a hot item. How come you didn't tell me?"

"Because it's not true!" I shouted. Two people huddled in the corner of the lunchroom looked up momentarily, then returned to their conversation. "Larry doesn't know what the hell he's talking about," I growled, more quietly.

"What's all the fuss, then?" she asked, her hands resting on her growing abdomen.

"I would just appreciate it if you wouldn't shout my business all over the place," I said. "What else did Larry tell you?"

"Just that you two look kinda cute together. I think he's right."

"Well, keep your goddamn thoughts to yourself." I stomped out of the lunchroom, angry all over again.

I crossed the hall to the new office area and found Urbin and Elmo uncrating burlap-covered wall-partition assemblies. They were dividing the various parts from the boxes and stacking them in piles. The partitions were a hideous bright orange. Without a word, I began to help them. When we had uncrated and stacked the last assembly, Elmo walked around the stacks with his engineer cap in his hand, scratching his head.

"How da hell are dese office folks s'posed ta concentrate when dey gotta stare at dis crappy color all day?" he asked nobody in particular.

Urbin shook his head and lit a cigarette. "Mmm," he said, picking at nothing underneath his fingernails. Urbin was the only workingman I knew who couldn't stand to get dirty. He worked hard, of course, and got as filthy as the rest of us. But as soon as he had a chance, he would run to the men's room and scrub everything he could with Lava.

I knew of no other man working at the gas company— including the janitors—who would pick the dead leaves off plants as he moved about from one office to the next. In fact, next to me he was the only one who seemed to give a damn about Gasco's dying foliage. Sometimes he would follow right behind me, picking at the itty-bitty dead leaves that I'd missed. Together we had probably pruned a thousand plants.

Urbin and Elmo eyeballed our project. Then Urbin picked up a set of instructions and began to read aloud: *A small amount of assembly required.* One of the scariest sentences in the world. As he read it, I knew we were in for a long day.

At noon I sat in the downstairs lunchroom and examined my damaged cuticles. I wasn't in the mood for socializing, and I knew that if I really wanted to avoid young Dick Carlson I should have gone to the ladies' rest room, or the second floor, or the truck, or anywhere else. But I didn't. I told myself that I was too tired to move. The servicemen's school let out, and the lunchroom became crowded and noisy.

"I'm glad you're here," Dick said, as he and Larry took the empty seats at my table. "A bunch of us are meeting after work on Friday to go dancing. Love to have you come with us, if you're free."

"Who's going?" Larry asked, butting in. I planned to talk to Larry about his blabbing to Sonny, but Dick's attentions were beginning to give Larry's insinuations some credibility. Or so I hoped.

"A few meter readers are going, I guess," Dick said. "Sue Anderson invited me. She said she talked to Lila, Judy, Julie, and Pam. Sonny, too, of course."

"Hell, Carlson," Larry blurted. "I'd better go, too. An innocent like you might need help with all those female types. Charlene and I'll chaperone."

Dick stared at him. "No need," he said, smiling, then looked at me, though his words were for Larry.

"By the way, Sonny tells me that you've been describing Peggie and me to the world as a *hot item*. At best, that seems a little premature, don't you think?"

Larry, for once, was speechless.

A year after Dick made his cautionary comment to Larry about our possible relationship, I asked Lenny if I could have a day off from work.

"What for?" he asked.

"I'm getting married."

"Monday?"

"Yeah."

"To who? Do I know the lucky guy?"

"Yes. You know him," I said, reluctantly. Lenny stared at his empty mug. I knew this was one secret I could no longer keep. "We haven't told anyone here yet, but it's Dick Carlson," I said, blushing like Lenny.

"That's great," Lenny said, happily. "He's a real good guy. You'll make a wonderful couple," Lenny wrinkled his nose with a look of concern. Now come the questions, I thought.

"You only want one day?"

On April 12, 1977, Richard and I (I didn't like the name Dick) got married. It was a practical-minded ceremony performed in Watertown, South Dakota, by a court clerk. His two secretaries were our only witnesses. The next day we went back to work. The following fall we bought a house, and Richard started law school.

Word of our marriage slowly made its way around Minnegasco. All the effort that we spent hoping to ward off the *objection* to our interracial union was, for the most part, wasted energy. Our friends congratulated us, and scolded us for keeping our courtship to ourselves.

Richard dedicated his days to Minnegasco and his nights to William Mitchell College of Law. Eventually, he traded his tool belt for a job in the public defender's office. I stayed at Minnegasco, mainly because I still did not know what I wanted to do with my life and because we suddenly had a lot of bills.

One morning in the early 1980s, Lenny gathered the Building and Grounds crew, as he always did. But I noticed he wasn't carrying any work orders.

"Ah, if I could have your attention for a minute?" he said.

Elmo was standing next to him, with his hair washed and parted as it usually was at the end of the day. Nobody was in a hurry, so Lenny had to wait for us to assemble.

"Some of you already know about this," Lenny said, putting an arm around Elmo. "Elmo has decided to retire."

A lump grew in my throat. I'd known this day was going to come sooner or later. But I didn't want it to be today, or any other day. I wasn't ready for a gas company without him.

Lenny was saying that he'd arranged a breakfast for the entire department, at Perkins, so that we could say our good-byes to him. Elmo, embarrassed, looked at his shoes.

Elmo's engineer cap sat on the folding table, but it looked different. It sparkled with recent laundering. It looked almost fluffy, standing at attention as if it were on display in a shop window.

I couldn't help myself. I walked over and threw my arms around him. "Elmo, I'm going to miss you," I whispered.

He smiled. "Dat dere's fer you," he said, pointing at the cap. "Da wife washed it up fer ya. Cleaned it up real goot."

"I can't take your cap," I said, trying to hold back tears.

"You gotta have a cap," he said. He put it on my head.

"Excuse me," I said, as I ran out to the yard to cry in private.

# Epilogue

MOM FELL IN LOVE WITH DICK. She denied having made derogatory remarks about Minnegasco employees. In 1979, on our second wedding anniversary, I gave birth to a beautiful baby girl, Jenna Nicole. Twelve years later, we adopted five-year-old Frankie and his stuffed dog, Bob. Whenever I referred to them as my children, Mom smiled and said, "Yes, dear. But they are *my* perfect grandchildren." Until her death in 1995, my mother was my best friend, biggest fan, and the pushiest supporter of my work.

Sonny had a blond, curly-haired boy named Jachai. I am his proud godmother. Sonny left Minnegasco, received a master's degree in social work, and went on to work for the state.

Dick left Minnegasco in 1980. I was promoted to foreman—at some point my title was changed to forewoman—and stayed until 1985.

# Acknowledgments

FROM THE BEGINNING, I knew that one day I would write a book about working at Minnegasco. I filled half a dozen journals in the eleven years I worked there. My brother Robert "accidentally" trashed the journals, but some things are unforgettable. And where memory failed me, the following folks stepped in to help set the record straight: Sue Anderson, Dick (the "Silver Fox") Carlson, Lucille Carlson, Randy Ferrian, Marty Hudja, Jolene ("Sonny") Kohn, Lenny Noren, Judy Olson, Steve (the "Sewer Man") Renkert, Julie Skaalerud, and John Trulen.

A special thanks is due to Urbin Mayer for gently reminding me, on more than one occasion, that his name is not spelled Urban Mayor.

I thank copy editor Lynn Marasco for her many helpful suggestions and skill with commas. Also, I wish to thank Ann Regan, managing editor of the Minnesota Historical Society Press, for having faith in this project. And thank you, Richard, Jenna, and Frankie for your support and patience while I worked on this book.

Finally, I wish to note that some names have been changed to protect the innocent—and the guilty. But the name Max "Elmo" Melbye will always be special to me.

*The Girls Are Coming* was designed and set in type by Will Powers at Minnesota Historical Society Press. The typeface is Chaparral, designed in 1997 by Carol Twombly. Printed by Maple-Vail Press.

CPSIA information can be obtained
at www.ICGtesting.com
Printed in the USA
JSHW021343200421
13748JS00001B/32